ROUGH GUIDES

POCKET **ROUGH GUIDE**

DUBAI

written and researched by

GAVIN THOMAS

CONTENTS

DUBAI

Dubai is like nowhere else on the planet. Often claimed to be the world's fastest-growing city, in the past five decades it has metamorphosed from a small Gulf trading centre to become one of the world's most glamorous, spectacular and futuristic urban destinations, fuelled by a heady cocktail of petrodollars, visionary commercial acumen and naked ambition. Dubai's ability to dream – and then achieve – the impossible has ripped up expectations and rewritten the record books, as evidenced by stunning developments such as the soaring Burj Khalifa, the beautiful Burj al Arab and the vast Palm Jumeirah island. Each is a remarkable testament to the ruling sheikhs' determination to make this one of the world's essential destinations for the twenty-first century.

Sheikh Zayed Road

Modern Dubai is often seen as a panegyric to consumerist luxury: a self-indulgent haven of magical hotels, superlative restaurants and extravagantly themed shopping malls. Perhaps not surprisingly the city is often stereotyped as a vacuous consumerist fleshpot, appealing only to those with more cash than culture, although this one-eyed cliché does absolutely no justice to Dubai's beguiling contrasts and rich cultural make-up. The city's headline-grabbing mega-projects have also deflected attention from Dubai's massive but largely unappreciated role in providing the Middle East with a model of political stability, religious tolerance and business acumen in action. In one of the world's most turbulent regions this peaceful and progressive pan-Arabian global city serves as the ultimate symbol of what can be achieved. Dubai also ranks among the world's most multicultural cities, featuring a cosmopolitan cast of Emiratis, Arabs, Iranians, Indians, Filipinos and Europeans – a fascinating patchwork of peoples and languages which gives the city its uniquely varied cultural appeal.

For the visitor, there's far more to Dubai than designer boutiques and five-star hotels – although of course if all you're looking for is a luxurious dose of sun, sand and shopping, the city takes some beating. Step beyond the tourist clichés, however, and you'll discover a multi-layered city full of contrasting cultures and futuristic daring – plus a fair dash of history too. The old city centre serves up many fascinating reminders of Dubai's past, including the grand old wind-towered mansions of Bastakiya and Shindagha; the stately wooden dhows which still moor up alongside the breezy Creek; and, of course, the helter-skelter souks of Bur Dubai and Deira, piled high with traditional Arabian jewellery, scents and spices – frankincense from Somalia, Bedouin necklaces from Oman, rose leaves from Iran. The city's modern attractions are equally memorable, ranging from world-famous contemporary icons like the futuristic Burj Khalifa, the world's tallest building, and the iconic, sail-shaped Burj al Arab through to myriad quirkier attractions – kitsch faux-Arabian bazaars, ersatz pyramids, zany

Antique Bazaar restaurant

Best places for a Dubai view

Dubai is the world's tallest city and getting your head in the clouds is all part of the experience. The "At the Top" tour to the stunning observation deck of the **Burj Khalifa** (see page 51) is unmissable, while there are further superlative panoramas from the Ain Dubai observation wheel and the Dubai Frame – not to mention a number of high-rise bars including **Bar 44** (see page 80), **Vault** (see page 59) and **Up on the Tenth** (see page 41).

Spice Souk

themed shopping malls and a string of other wonderful, wacky and sometimes downright weird modern landmarks. In addition, Dubai is within easy striking distance of a number of other rewarding day-trip destinations, including Sharjah, home to some fine museums, the laidback inland oasis city of Al Ain and the vibrant megalopolis of Abu Dhabi, capital of the UAE.

After years of retrenchment following the 2008 credit crunch (during which Dubai teetered perilously on the brink of bankruptcy) the city is now back on the rise, epitomized by its hosting of the gargantuan Expo 2020, while other landmark recent openings have included the stunningly outlandish Museum of the Future and the frankly bizarre Dubai Frame, not to mention completion of the long-awaited Dubai Water Canal. Pronouncements of the city's demise have proved decidedly premature, and Dubai remains one of the twenty-first century's most fascinating and vibrant urban experiments. This is where you can literally see history in the making.

When to visit

The best time to visit Dubai is in the cooler winter months from December through to February, with average daily temperatures in the mid-20s Temperatures rise significantly from March through to April, and in October and November, when the thermometer regularly nudges up into the 30s. From May to September the city boils – July and August are especially suffocating – with average temperatures in the high 30s to low 40s (and frequently higher). Room rates at most of the top hotels fall during this period, sometimes dramatically, making the summer an excellent time to enjoy some authentic Dubaian luxury at relatively affordable prices. Rainfall is rare for most of the year, although there are usually a few wet days during January and February.

Where to...

Shop

Shopping in Dubai takes two forms. First, there are the old-fashioned souks of **Bur Dubai**, **Karama** and **Deira**, good for traditional items like gold, perfume and spices (not to mention designer fakes). Bargaining is the norm for most items. Then there's the city's spectacular collection of supersized malls. Head to the **Dubai Mall** for the ultimate retail experience, while the sprawling **Mall of the Emirates** is another must-shop. More manageable retail destinations include the **BurJuman**, **Mercato** and **Marina** malls and **Wafi**.

OUR FAVOURITES: Gold Souk, see page 34, Souk Madinat Jumeirah, see page 67, Ajmal, see page 31.

Eat

It's almost impossible not to eat well in Dubai, whatever your budget. There's inexpensive food galore in the curry houses of **Bur Dubai** and **Karama** and at the shwarma stands and Lebanese-style cafés of **Deira**, **Satwa** and elsewhere, while both home-grown and international cafés and fast-food chains citywide provide further affordable options. Most of the city's more upscale restaurants are located in hotels – many of the best can be found in **Sheikh Zayed Road/Downtown Dubai**, or along the coast in the **Dubai Marina** or around the **Burj al Arab**.

OUR FAVOURITES: Pierchic, see page 69, Eazone, see page 79, Rockfish, see page 70.

Drink

You won't go thirsty in Dubai, although alcohol is only served in hotel bars, pubs and restaurants. You'll come across British-style **pubs**, complete with pints and inexpensive counter food alongside swanky **cocktail bars**, many situated in skyscrapers with spectacular views. And then there are the more romantic beachside and Arabian-style places perfect for date nights around the **Burj al Arab**, **Dubai Marina** and the **Palm Jumeirah**. Alcohol doesn't come cheap, although most places run some kind of **happy hour**. In addition, many places also host regular **ladies' nights** (usually Tuesday or Wednesday) offering women complimentary or heavily discounted tipples.

OUR FAVOURITES: Bartasti Bar, see page 80, Bahri bar, see page 71, Skyview Bar, see page 71.

Go out

Nightlife in Dubai takes various forms. Locals tend to hit the city's myriad **malls**, which stay open till late and remain busy right up until midnight. Visitors usually head for the city's **restaurants** and **bars** – many of the latter host regular live music or DJs – while it's also fun to hang out in a **shisha café**. There's a growing number of **clubs**, although many places are more about pouting and posing than partying. Cultural events are a bit thin on the ground, outside of the annual Dubai jazz and film **festivals**.

OUR FAVOURITES: Creek View Restaurant, see page 41, B018 Dubai, see page 81, Rooftop Terrace, see page 81.

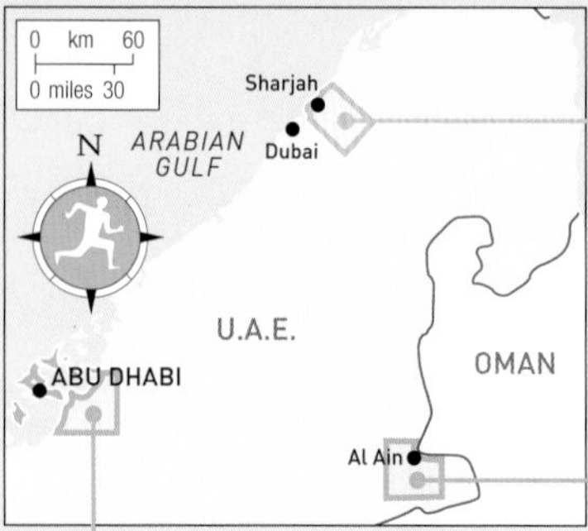

Sharjah p.82.

Just up the coast from Dubai, conservative Sharja
is home to the country's m
rewarding cluster of muse

Al Ain p.86.

The UAE's largest inland ci
dotted with lush oases and
mud-brick forts beneath th
craggy summit of Jebel Ha

Abu Dhabi p.90.

Capital of the UAE and home to a string of attractions ranging from the futuristic Al Maryah Island to the opulent Sheikh Zayed Mosque.

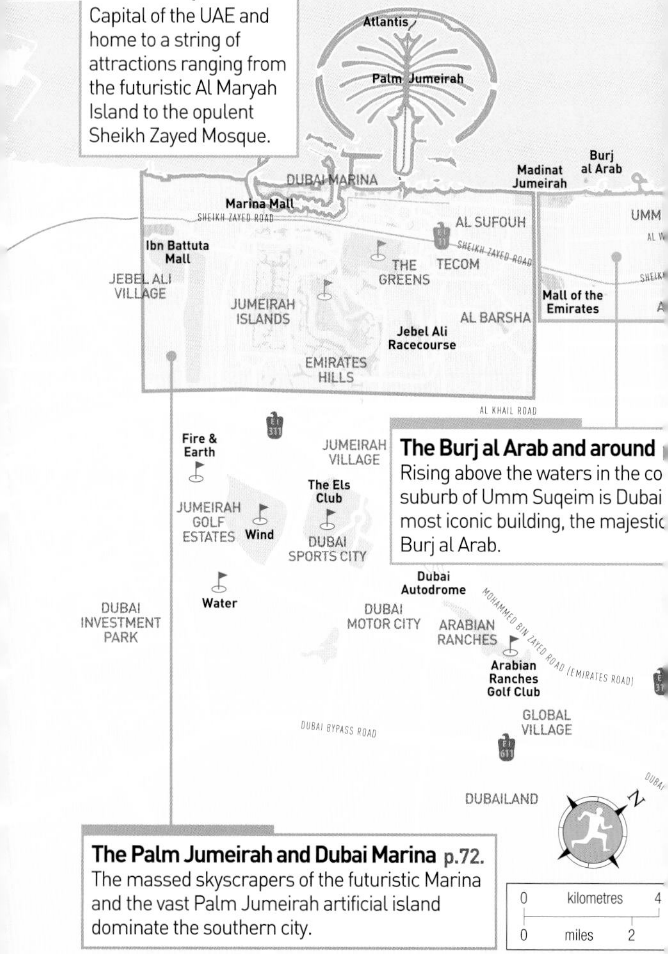

The Burj al Arab and around

Rising above the waters in the co
suburb of Umm Suqeim is Dubai
most iconic building, the majestic
Burj al Arab.

The Palm Jumeirah and Dubai Marina p.72.

The massed skyscrapers of the futuristic Marina and the vast Palm Jumeirah artificial island dominate the southern city.

Dubai at a glance

Deira p.34.
An endless sprawl of souks piled high with everything from gold, spices and perfumes to laptops, tablets and mobile phones.

Bur Dubai p.24.
The old heart of Dubai, with souks, mosques and traditional wind-towered houses lined up alongside the breezy Creek.

eirah p.60.
of Dubai's most exclusive suburbs, a few low-key sights dotted among awling expanse of upmarket villas.

ikh Zayed Road Downtown Dubai p.50.
ai in the sky: from the towering -rises of Sheikh Zayed Road to oaring Burj Khalifa.

inner suburbs p.42.
rasting suburbs and sights ring ld city centre, ranging from ımarket Karama to the chic ern developments of Oud Metha.

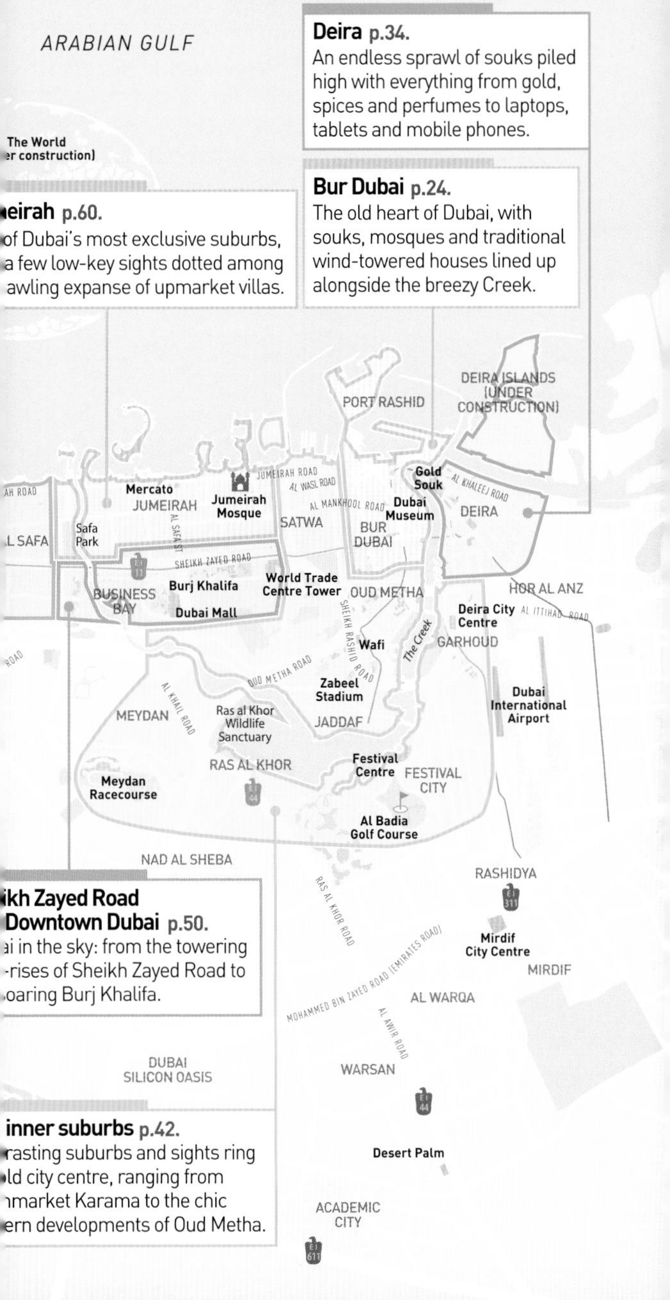

15 Things not to miss

It's not always possible to see everything that Dubai has to offer in one trip, especially if you are only visiting for a few days. What follows is a selective taste of the emirate's highlights, from the best souks to unmissable activities and some of the world's most staggering architectural accomplishments.

> **Burj al Arab**
See page 64
Superb, sail-shaped hotel towering above the coast of southern Dubai.

< **Burj Khalifa**
See page 51
The world's tallest building, rising like an enormous space rocket above Downtown Dubai.

∨ **Deira souks**
See page 34
An intricate tangle of bazaars piled high with gold, spices, perfumes and more.

< **Museum of the Future**

See page 50

This innovative doughnut-shaped museum is one of city's most arresting landmarks.

∨ **Gold Souk**

See page 34

Dubai's most dazzling souk. Everything here glitters, and it really is gold.

< **Dubai Frame**

See page 45

Surreal picture frame-shaped "building" with peerless city views.

∨ **Jumeirah Mosque**

See page 60

Dubai's most beautiful mosque – open to visitors during informative guided tours.

∧ **Al Shindgha Museum**

See page 29

Ancient and modern meet at this state-of-the-art new heritage museum.

< **Sheikh Saeed al Maktoum House**

See page 29

Former home of the ruling sheikhs, now an absorbing museum.

∧ **Dhow Wharfage**

See page 37

Dozens of superb Arabian dhows moored up along the Deira Creekside.

∨ **One&Only Royal Mirage**

See page 104

Dubai's most romantic hotel, with gorgeous Moorish decor and palm trees galore.

∧ **Desert Safaris**

See page 112

A desert safari with camel rides, traditional tents and miles of rolling dunes is a fun trip. Make it extra special and stay overnight.

< **Sheikh Zayed Mosque, Abu Dhabi**

See page 94

Magnificent modern mosque, with a spectacularly opulent prayer hall within.

< **Sharjah Museum of Islamic Civilization**

See page 82

State-of-the-art museum showcasing the history, arts and scientific contributions of the Islamic world.

∨ **Al Ain Oasis**

See page 86

Shady plantations of luxuriant date palms in the heart of Al Ain.

Day One in Dubai

Deira Gold Souk. See page 34. Browse the shop windows of Deira's most famous souk, stuffed with vast quantities of gold and precious stones.

Dhow Wharfage. See page 37. A little slice of living maritime history, with dozens of antique wooden dhows moored up alongside the Creek.

Cross the Creek by abra. See page 29. Jump on board one of these old-fashioned wooden ferries for the memorable short crossing to Bur Dubai.

Lunch. See page 32. Relax over a light lunch in the beautiful garden of the *Arabian Tea House Café*.

Bastakiya. See page 25. Get lost amid the winding alleyways and wind-towered houses of Dubai's most perfectly preserved old quarter and have a look at quaint Al Fahidi Fort the city's oldest building (home to the – currently closed – Dubai Museum).

A walk along the Creek. See page 24. Walk past the Grand Mosque and through the Textile Souk and out along the breezy creekside to Shindagha.

Sheikh Saeed al Maktoum House. See page 29. A fascinating collection of historical photographs showcases the rapidly changing face of Dubai.

Al Shindagha Museum. See page 29. Explore the myriad galleries of this superb new heritage museum, showcasing the myriad riches of Dubai's traditional culture.

Dinner. See page 33. Settle down for a supper of superb traditional Arabian cuisine at *Al Khayma Heritage Restaurant*.

Traditional dhow on the Creek

Bastakiya

Along the Creek to Al Shindagha

Day Two in Dubai

Walk down Sheikh Zayed Road. See page 50. Start at the stunning Emirates Towers and landmark Museum of the Future and then wander south along Sheikh Zayed Road, Dubai's most flamboyantly futuristic architectural parade.

At the Top, Burj Khalifa. See page 51. Ride the world's fastest elevators to the spectacular observation deck on the 124th floor of the world's tallest building.

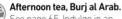

Lunch. See page 56. Explore the myriad culinary offerings on show at the Time Out Market, showcasing some of the best cooking in the city.

Dubai Mall. See page 53. Dive into the city's mall to end all malls, offering endless hours of retail therapy and a host of other entertainments.

Afternoon tea, Burj al Arab. See page 65. Indulge in an opulent afternoon tea in the iconic, "seven-star" Burj al Arab's *Sahn Eddar* lounge.

Souk Madinat Jumeirah. See page 67. Walk over to the stunning Madinat Jumeirah complex, with its picture-perfect waterways and old-fashioned souk.

Dinner. See page 69. Eat a memorable meal above the Madinat waterways at the gorgeously romantic *Pai Thai*, then head off for a night of clubbing at the kicking *BO18* club.

View from the Burj Khalifa

Souk Madinat Jumeirah

Pai Thai

Souks and shopping

For a taste of retail therapy, Dubai style, you'll need to explore both the city's traditional souks and its shiny modern malls.

Gold Souk. See page 34. Haggle for bangles, bracelets and necklaces at Deira's bustling Gold Souk.

Spice Souk. See page 35. Shop for Middle Eastern spices, frankincense and more at the city's photogenic Spice Souk.

Perfume Souk. See page 37. Check out the local and international scents – or make up your own bespoke fragrance.

Wafi. See page 42. One of the city's smoothest shopping experiences with one of the city's coolest collections of independent fashion labels.

Khan Murjan Souk. See page 42. Explore the myriad shops of the pretty Khan Murjan, bursting with Arabian scents, jewellery, textiles, furniture and much more.

Lunch. See page 48. The enjoyable *Khan Murjan Restaurant* serves up Middle Eastern cuisine in a good-looking outdoor courtyard.

Mall of the Emirates. See page 67. Perhaps the city's most satisfying all-in-one retail destination, with 500-odd shops to explore.

Ibn Battuta Mall. See page 78. Catch the metro down to Dubai's most eye-catching mall, extravagantly themed after Ibn Battuta's travels.

Dinner. See page 78. Have dinner at the spectacular *Buddha Bar*, with crisp cocktails, Asian fine-dining and one of the city's most flamboyant interiors.

Gold Souk

Perfume Souk

Mall of the Emirates

Hidden Dubai

To escape the crowds, head for some of Dubai's less well-known attractions – although you'll need a car or taxi for the latter part of the day.

Naif Museum. See page 38. This little-visited museum showcases the engaging history of the Dubai police force since colonial times.

Al Wasl and Covered souks. See page 37. Walk down Al Musallah Street then dive west into the tangle of little streets and alleyways of the disorienting Al Wasl Souk.

Hindi Lane. See page 27. Take an abra across the Creek to Bur Dubai's Textile Souk, just a few steps from this entertaining little Indian enclave of Hindi Lane.

Lunch. See page 32. The lovely little *XVA Café* is close to Hindi Lane, tucked away at the back of Bastakiya.

Iranian mosques. See page 28. It's a short walk through the Textile Souk to Bur Dubai's fine pair of Iranian Shia'a mosques.

Ras al Khor Wildlife Sanctuary. See page 46. Take a taxi out to the Ras al Khor Wildlife Sanctuary, with flocks of vivid pink flamingoes incongruously framed against distant skyscrapers.

Majlis Ghorfat um al Sheif. See page 62. This picturesque old mud-brick house is incongruously marooned amid the villas of Jumeirah.

Dinner. See page 47. Grab a pavement table at the always bustling *Al Mallah* Lebanese café in the personable suburb of Satwa, a part of the city usually overlooked by tourists.

Naif Museum

Ras Al Khor Wildlife Sanctuary

Iranian Mosque

PLACES

Marina beach

Bur Dubai

Strung out along the southern side of the Creek, Bur Dubai is the oldest part of the city. Parts of the district's historic waterfront still retain their engagingly old-fashioned appearance, with a quaint tangle of sand-coloured buildings and a distinctively Arabian skyline, spiked with dozens of wind towers and the occasional minaret. At the heart of the district the absorbing Dubai Museum offers an excellent introduction to the city's history, while the old Iranian quarter of Bastakiya is home to its most impressive collection of traditional buildings. Heading west along the Creek, the old-fashioned Textile Souk is the prettiest in the city, while further along the waterfront the historic quarter of Shindagha is home to another fine cluster of century-old edifices and the superb new Al Shindagha Museum.

The Creek

MAP P.26, POCKET MAP M11–N10

Cutting a broad, salty swathe through the middle of the city centre, **the Creek** (Al Khor in Arabic) lies physically and historically at the very heart of Dubai. The Creek was the location of the earliest settlements in the area – first on the Bur Dubai side of the water, and subsequently in Deira – and also played a crucial role in establishing Dubai as a major port during the twentieth

The Creek

century. Commerce aside, the Creek remains the centrepiece of Dubai and its finest natural feature; a broad, serene stretch of water which is as essential a part of the fabric and texture of the city as the Thames is to London or the Seine to Paris.

The walk along the Bur Dubai waterfront is particularly lovely, pedestrianized throughout, and with cooling breezes and wonderful views of the city down the Creek – particularly beautiful towards sunset. For the best views, begin in Shindagha (see page 29) and head south. It takes about twenty minutes to reach Bastakiya, from where you can continue into the new Al Seef development. A spacious promenade stretches down the waterfront as far as Shindagha Tower, from where a narrow walkway extends down to the Bur Dubai Abra Station and the Textile Souk.

Dubai Museum

MAP P.26, POCKET MAP M12
Al Fahidi St. Al Fahidi metro, www.visitdubai.com/en/places-to-visit/dubai-museum.

At the dead centre of Bur Dubai stands the old **Al Fahidi Fort**, a rough-and-ready little structure whose engagingly lopsided corner turrets – one square and one round – make it look a bit like a giant sandcastle. Dating from around 1800, the fort is the oldest building in Dubai, having originally been built to defend the town's landward approaches against raids by rival Bedouin tribes. It also served as the residence and office of the ruling sheikh up until the early twentieth century before being converted into a museum in 1971. **Dubai Museum**, however, has been closed for renovations for several years now, with no reopening date announced.

Bastakiya

MAP P.26, POCKET MAP N12
Sharaf DG metro. Coins Museum. Coffee Museum coffeemuseum.ae, free.

Bastakiya

Architectural Heritage Department, free. Majlis Gallery, themajlisgallery.com.

The beautiful old quarter of **Bastakiya** (also often described as Al Fahidi Historical Neighbourhood) comprises a photogenic huddle of traditional Gulf houses, capped with dozens of wind towers and arranged around a rabbit warren of tiny alleyways.

A number of old Bastakiya houses have now been opened to the public as small-scale museums and galleries. Best is the quaint little **Coffee Museum**, stuffed full of antique coffee-making paraphernalia and other artefacts from around the world. Also worth a look are the **Coins Museum**, containing a well-presented collection of over four hundred Islamic coins, and the **Architectural Heritage Department**, boasting a particularly large and chintzy courtyard and fine views over Bastakiya from its roof. Nearby is the long-running **Majlis Gallery**, the oldest in the city, founded in 1989 and hosting monthly exhibitions showcasing the work of Emirati and international artists.

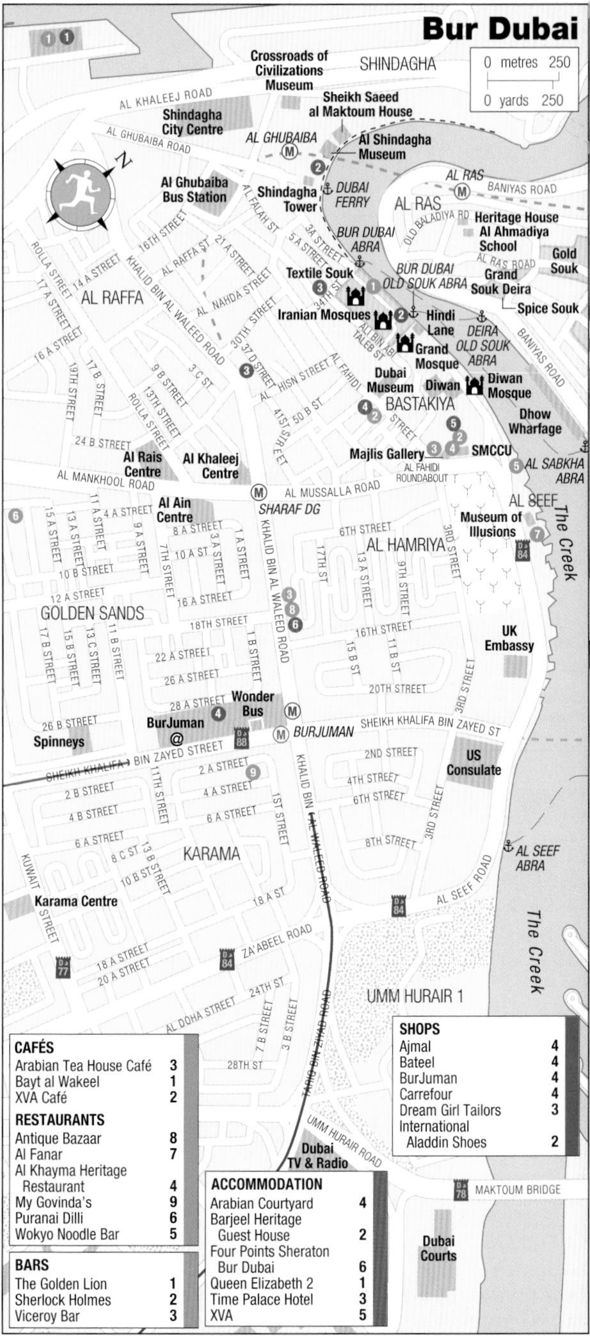
Bur Dubai
0 metres 250
0 yards 250
SHINDAGHA
Crossroads of Civilizations Museum
Sheikh Saeed al Maktoum House
Al Shindagha Museum
AL KHALEEJ ROAD
AL GHUBAIBA ROAD
Shindagha City Centre
AL GHUBAIBA
Al Ghubaiba Bus Station
Shindagha Tower
DUBAI FERRY
AL RAS
BANIYAS ROAD
AL RAS
Heritage House
Al Ahmadiya School
Gold Souk
BUR DUBAI ABRA
BUR DUBAI OLD SOUK ABRA
Grand Souk Deira
Spice Souk
Textile Souk
Iranian Mosques
Hindi Lane
DEIRA OLD SOUK ABRA
Grand Mosque
Dubai Museum
Diwan
Diwan Mosque
BASTAKIYA
Dhow Wharfage
Majlis Gallery
SMCCU
AL FAHIDI ROUNDABOUT
AL SABKHA ABRA
AL RAFFA
KHALID BIN AL WALEED ROAD
Al Rais Centre
Al Khaleej Centre
AL MANKHOOL ROAD
AL MUSSALLA ROAD
SHARAF DG
Al Ain Centre
AL HAMRIYA
AL SEEF
Museum of Illusions
The Creek
GOLDEN SANDS
UK Embassy
Wonder Bus
BurJuman
BURJUMAN
Spinneys
SHEIKH KHALIFA BIN ZAYED ST
US Consulate
KARAMA
Karama Centre
AL SEEF ABRA
AL SEEF ROAD
ZA'ABEEL ROAD
UMM HURAIR 1
AL DOHA STREET
TARIQ BIN ZIYAD ROAD
UMM HURAIR ROAD
Dubai TV & Radio
MAKTOUM BRIDGE
Dubai Courts
CAFÉS
Arabian Tea House Café 3
Bayt al Wakeel 1
XVA Café 2
RESTAURANTS
Antique Bazaar 8
Al Fanar 7
Al Khayma Heritage Restaurant 4
My Govinda's 9
Puranai Dilli 6
Wokyo Noodle Bar 5
BARS
The Golden Lion 1
Sherlock Holmes 2
Viceroy Bar 3
ACCOMMODATION
Arabian Courtyard 4
Barjeel Heritage Guest House 2
Four Points Sheraton Bur Dubai 6
Queen Elizabeth 2 1
Time Palace Hotel 3
XVA 5
SHOPS
Ajmal 4
Bateel 4
BurJuman 4
Carrefour 4
Dream Girl Tailors 3
International Aladdin Shoes 2

Wind towers

Often described as the world's oldest form of air-conditioning, the distinctive **wind towers** (*barjeel*) that top many old Dubai buildings (as well as numerous modern ones constructed in faux-Arabian style) provided an ingeniously simple way of countering the Gulf's searing temperatures in a pre-electrical age. Rising around 6m (20ft) above the rooftops on which they're built, wind towers are open on all four sides and channel any available breezes down into the building via triangular flues. Bastakiya's collection of wind towers is the largest and finest in the city, with subtle variations in design from tower to tower, meaning that no two are ever exactly alike.

The SMCCU

MAP P.26, POCKET MAP N12
Near Al Fahidi Roundabout. Sharaf DG metro, ⓦ cultures.ae.

Based in an office on the eastern edge of Bastakiya, the pioneering **Sheikh Mohammed Centre for Cultural Understanding**, or **SMCCU**, runs popular tours of Jumeirah Mosque (see page 60) and a number of activities in Bastakiya itself, including **walking tours**, Gulf Arabic classes and "cultural" breakfasts and lunches, during which you get the chance to sample some traditional food while chatting to the centre's Emirati staff.

The Grand Mosque and Diwan

MAP P.26, POCKET MAP M11 & N12
Next to the Al Fahidi Fort, Ali bin Abi Taleb St. Sharaf DG metro. No entry to non-Muslims.

Dubai's grandest place of worship, the imposing **Grand Mosque** is an impressively large if rather plain structure, the general austerity relieved only by an elaborate swirl of Koranic script over the entrance and the city's tallest minaret. Hugging the creekside immediately east of the Grand Mosque sits the **Diwan**, or Ruler's Court, now home to assorted government functionaries, and the eye-catching **Diwan Mosque**, topped by an unusually flattened onion dome and a slender white minaret which rivals that of the nearby Grand Mosque in height.

The Textile Souk

MAP P.26, POCKET MAP M11
Al Ghubaiba metro.

At the heart of Bur Dubai, the **Textile Souk** (also sometimes referred to as the "Old Souk") is easily the prettiest in the city, occupying an immaculately restored traditional bazaar, its long line of sand-coloured buildings shaded by a fine arched wooden roof, pleasantly cool even in the heat of the day and illuminated by traditional Moorish hanging lights after dark. This was once the most important bazaar in the city although its commercial importance has long since faded and almost all the shops have now been taken over by Indian traders flogging reams of sari cloth and fluorescent blankets, alongside assorted tourist tat. If you're hankering after an I ♥ DUBAI T-shirt or spangly camel, now's your chance.

Hindi Lane

MAP P.26, POCKET MAP M11
Textile Souk. Sharaf DG metro.

The colourful little alleyway popularly known as **Hindi Lane** is one of Dubai's most curious and appealing little ethnic enclaves. Walk to the far (eastern) end of the Textile Souk, turn right by T.

Textile Souk

Singh Trading and then left by Shubham Textiles and you'll find yourself in a tiny alleyway lined with picturesque little Indian shops selling an array of bangles, bindis, coconuts, flowers, bells, almanacs and other religious paraphernalia. On the north side of Hindi Lane is the tiny hybridized Hindu-cum-Sikh temple sometimes referred to as the **Sikh Gurudaba**, while continuing along Hindi Lane to the back of the Grand Mosque brings you to a second Hindu temple, the **Shri Nathji Temple**, dedicated to Krishna.

Iranian mosques

MAP P.26, POCKET MAP M11
Ali bin Abi Taleb St (11c St). Al Ghubaiba metro. No entry to non-Muslims.

Hidden away on the south side of the Textile Souk are two of the city's finest **Iranian mosques**. The more easterly of the two mosques is particularly eye-catching, with a superb facade and dome covered in a lustrous mosaic of predominantly blue tiling decorated with geometrical floral motifs. The second mosque, about 50m (164ft) west along the road, close to the *Time Palace Hotel*, is a contrastingly plain, sand-coloured building, its rooftop enlivened by four tightly packed little egg-shaped domes.

Al Fahidi Street

MAP P.26, POCKET MAP M11–N12
Sharaf DG and BurJuman metros.

Al Fahidi Street is Bur Dubai's de facto high street, lined with a mix of shops selling Indian clothing, shoes and jewellery along with other places stacked high with mobile phones and fancy watches (not necessarily genuine). The eastern end of the street and adjacent Al Hisn Street are also often loosely referred to as **Meena Bazaar**, the centre of the district's textile and tailoring industry and home to a dense razzle-dazzle of shopfronts stuffed with sumptuous saris.

Al Seef

MAP P.26, POCKET MAP N12–N13
Museum of Illusions,
Ⓦ museumofillusions.ae, charge.

West of Bastakiya, **Al Seef** district meanders alongside the Creekside waterfront for over a kilometre. The area's canopied alleyways, quaint squares and wind-towered traditional houses look as old as anything in the city but are in fact entirely modern, the entire "historic" district having been dreamt up by property developers Meraas and opened in 2017. It's not exactly authentic, but makes an attractive place for idle wandering, pedestrianized throughout and with dozens of small shops and cafes to explore, as well as the entertaining **Museum of Illusions**, home to a diverting array of brain-twisting exhibits.

Shindagha

MAP P.26, POCKET MAP M10–N10

Although now effectively swallowed up by Bur Dubai, the historic creekside district of **Shindagha** was, until fifty years ago, a quite separate and self-contained area occupying its own spit of land, and frequently cut off from Bur Dubai proper during high tides. This was once the most exclusive address in town, home to the ruling family and other local elites, who occupied a series of imposing houses lined up along the waterfront. The edge of the district is guarded by the distinctive waterfront **Shindagha Tower**, instantly recognizable thanks to the slit windows and protruding buttress on each side, arranged to resemble a human face.

Sheikh Saeed al Maktoum House

MAP P.26, POCKET MAP M10
Shindagha waterfront. Al Ghubaiba metro ⓣ 04 226 0286, charge.

Standing on the beautiful Shindagha waterfront, the **Sheikh Saeed al Maktoum House** is one of Dubai's most interesting museums, occupying what from 1896 to 1958 was the principal residence of Dubai's ruling family – an atmospheric wind-towered mansion arranged around a spacious sandy courtyard. Inside, pride of place goes to the superb collection of old **photographs**, with images of the city from the 1940s through to the late 1960s, showing the first steps in its amazing transformation from a remote Gulf town to global megalopolis.

Al Shindagha Museum

MAP P.26, POCKET MAP M10
Shindagha waterfront. Al Ghubaiba metro, ⓦ www.visitdubai.com/en/places-to-visit/al-shindagha-museum, charge.

Crossing the Creek by abra

One of the most fun things you can do in Bur Dubai is go for a ride by abra (see page 110) across the Creek – the area's two main abra stations are the **Bur Dubai Abra Station**, just outside the main entrance to the Textile Souk, and **Bur Dubai Old Souk Abra Station**, inside the souk itself, from where these old-fashioned little wooden boats shuttle across the Creek at all hours of the day and night to **Deira Old Souk** and **Al Sabkha** abra stations on the other side of the water in Deira (there are two further stations – Al Fahidi and Al Seef – further down the Creek either side of the new Al Seef development). The boats' basic design has changed little for at least a century, apart from the addition of a diesel engine, and abras still play a crucial role in the city's transport infrastructure, carrying a staggering twenty million passengers per year for a few dirham per trip.

Al Shindagha Museum

The newest and most ambitious of Bur Dubai's many heritage attractions, **Al Shindagha Museum** showcases the city's old traditions and spectacular modern transformation in an impressive series of state-of-the-art multimedia displays spread across an interlinked cluster of traditional houses. Ongoing plans aim to expand the complex into the UAE's largest heritage museum and you'll need at least a couple of hours here to even scrape of the surfaces of the exhibits so far opened, with individual pavilions dedicated to themes including perfume, medicine, jewellery, food, poetry and so on – or try your hand at some traditional embroidery or working a loom.

Heritage and Diving Villages

MAP P.26, POCKET MAP N10

Shindagha waterfront. Al Ghubaiba metro, free.

The so-called **Heritage Village** comprises a string of traditional buildings surrounding a large sandy courtyard, with a few souvenir shops at the back. The atmosphere is fairly moribund at most times, but livens up somewhat after dark during national holidays and festivals, when locals put on cookery and craft displays. The adjacent **Diving Village** offers more of the same, with further traditional buildings around another courtyard dotted with a couple of wooden boats and a few *barasti* huts.

Crossroads of Civilizations Museum

MAP P.26, POCKET MAP M10

Al Khaleej Road. Al Ghubaiba Metro, ⓦ themuseum.ae, charge.

Hidden away at the back of the Shindagha, this excellent museum showcases a small but spectacular array of mainly Middle Eastern artefacts. Highlights include some marvellously well-preserved Sumerian and Babylonian statuettes and a superb piece of *kiswah* (the cloth used to cover the Ka'aba in Mecca) donated by the great Ottoman ruler Suleiman the Magnificent.

Shops

Ajmal

MAP P.26, POCKET MAP M3

BurJuman. BurJuman metro, Ⓦ en-ae.ajmal.com.

Dubai's leading perfumiers, offering a wide range of fragrances including traditional *attar*-based Arabian scents. If you don't like any of their ready-made perfumes you can make up your own from the big glass bottles on display behind the counter. Numerous other branches across the city including at Deira Gold Souk, Deira City Centre, Dubai Mall and Mall of the Emirates.

Bateel

MAP P.26, POCKET MAP M3

BurJuman. BurJuman metro, Ⓦ bateel.com.

The best dates in the city, grown in Bateel's own plantations in Saudi Arabia and sold either plain, covered in chocolate or stuffed with ingredients such as almonds and slices of lemon or orange. Other branches at Deira City Centre, Souk al Bahar, Dubai Mall and Mall of the Emirates.

BurJuman

MAP P.26, POCKET MAP M3

Corner of Khalid bin al Waleed and Sheikh Zayed roads. BurJuman metro (exit 3), Ⓦ burjuman.com.

The biggest and best city-centre mall, BurJuman remains popular thanks to its convenient location, 300-plus shops plus a good spread of cafes and restaurants.

Carrefour

MAP P.26, POCKET MAP M3

BurJuman. BurJuman metro, Ⓦ carrefouruae.com.

This vast French hypermarket chain might not be the most atmospheric place to shop in the city, but is one of the best places to pick up just about any kind of Middle Eastern foodstuff you fancy, from cut-price dates to Yemeni honey. Other branches citywide including Deira City Centre, Mall of the Emirates and Marina Mall.

Dream Girl Tailors

MAP P.26, POCKET MAP L12

37d Street. Sharaf DG metro, Ⓦ dreamgirltailors.com.

Perhaps the best of the various tailors hereabouts, offering well-made, inexpensive copies of any existing garment you might bring in: around 85dh for a shirt or trousers, or from 200dh for a dress (not including material). They can also make up clothes from photographs or even a hand-drawn design. Other branches in Karama and Satwa.

International Aladdin Shoes

MAP P.26, POCKET MAP M11

Textile Souk (next to Bur Dubai Old Souk Abra Station). Al Ghubaiba metro, Ⓣ 050 744 6543.

Eye-catching little stall (no sign) in the midst of the Textile Souk selling a gorgeous selection of colourful embroidered ladies' slippers (from 60dh) along with embroidered belts.

Bateel dates

Arabian Tea House Café

Cafés

Arabian Tea House Café

MAP P.26, POCKET MAP N12
Al Fahidi St, next to the main entrance to Bastakiya. Sharaf DG metro, Ⓦ arabianteahouse.com.
Lovely little courtyard café set in the idyllic garden of a traditional old Bastakiya house. The menu features a good range of sandwiches and salads, plus assorted Arabian-style breakfasts and mains and a good choice of juices and coffees. DhDh

Bayt Al Wakeel

MAP P.26, POCKET MAP M11
Mackenzie House, near the main entrance to the Textile Souk. Al Ghubaiba metro, Ⓦ wakeel.ae.
The small menu of rather pedestrian Arabian food (plus some pricier seafood options) won't win any awards, but the convenient location near the entrance to the Textile Souk and the setting by the historic Mackenzie House on an attractive terrace jutting out into the Creek amply compensate. DhDh

XVA Café

MAP P.26, POCKET MAP N12
Bastakiya. Sharaf DG metro, Ⓦ xvahotel.com.
Tucked away in an alley at the back of Bastakiya, this shady courtyard café (attached to a lovely guesthouse; see page 99) serves up good meat-free meals with a Middle Eastern or Indian twist including flavoursome salads and sandwiches and a small selection of light meals , plus good breakfasts. DhDh

Restaurants

Antique Bazaar

MAP P.26, POCKET MAP M13
Four Points Sheraton, Khalid bin al Waleed Rd. Sharaf DG metro, Ⓦ antiquebazaar-dubai.com.
This pretty little restaurant, littered with assorted subcontinental artefacts, dishes up a fair selection of North Indian favourites with reasonable aplomb. There's also a decent resident band and dancers nightly from 9pm. DhDh

Al Fanar

MAP P.26, POCKET MAP N13
Al Seef. Sharaf DG metro, Ⓦ www.alfanarrestaurant.com/uae/al-seef.
On the waterfront in the new Al Seef development, this faux-antique restaurant offers beautiful views from its breezy Creekside terrace alongside one of the old city's best seafood menus (mains from 75dh)

including traditional dishes like fish/shrimp machboos and *jesheed* (minced shark). There are further Arabian favourites on the all-day breakfast menu – try the classic Gulf-style *balalit*, cardomom-flavoured vermicelli noodles with omelette and bread. DhDhDh

Al Khayma Heritage Restaurant

MAP P.26, POCKET MAP N12
Bastakiya. Sharaf DG metro, ⓦ alkhayma.com.
One of Dubai's best places to explore quality Middle Eastern and Gulf cuisine. The extensive menu features tasty breakfasts (try the classic Gulf-style *luqaimat* – sticky miniature dumplings served with *regag* flatbread) alongside salads, mezze and a good range of Arabian mains including traditional dishes like *machboos* – a kind of Gulf-style biryani. DhDhDh

My Govinda's

MAP P.26, POCKET MAP M3
4A St. BurJuman metro, ⓦ www.mygovindas.com.
One of Bur Dubai's longest-running Indian establishments, My Govinda's serves up top-notch pure vegetarian food at cut-throat prices including street food classics like bhel puri and aloo chaat alongside all sorts of veg mains and delicately spiced biryanis. Round things off with a scoop of one of the restaurant's twenty-odd natural ice cream flavours. Good mocktail list, too, but no alcohol. Dh

Purani Dilli

MAP P.26, POCKET MAP L2
4C St. Sharaf DG metro, ⓦ www.puranidillidubai.com.
"The flavours of Old Delhi" is the theme at this leading Indian restaurant, inspired by the classic Mughlai dishes of northern India and offering a wide range of richly flavoured tandooris and kebabs accompanied by sumptuous naans, rotis and parathas – plus a decent vegetarian selection. DhDhDh

Wokyo Noodle Bar

MAP P.26, POCKET MAP N12
Al Seef. Sharaf DG metro, ⓦ www.wokyo.com.
Located on the Al Seef waterfront, this Japanese-style noodle bar offers a flavoursome array of stir-fries, ramen noodle soups and Malay-style *laksas* for a tasty lunch or casual dinner. Dh

Bars

The Golden Lion

MAP P.26, POCKET MAP L1
Port Rashid. Al Ghubaiba metro. ⓦ qe2.com
Classic old-school British drinking establishment aboard the famous *QE2* cruise liner (see page 98), now rather cheekily billing itself as "Dubai's oldest pub", even though it only opened in the city in 2018. Inside, the décor features plenty of designer-free clunky wooden tables and plush velvet velour, with live sports on TV, pub grub and pints at 55dh, although the main attraction is obviously the chance to sup aboard this historic old vessel and have a nose around whilst on board.

Sherlock Holmes

MAP P.26, POCKET MAP M12
Arabian Courtyard Hotel, Al Fahidi St. Sharaf DG metro ⓣ 04 351 9111.
One of Bur Dubai's better pubs, with a relaxed atmosphere, flock wallpaper and glass cases full of vaguely Sherlock Holmes-related memorabilia – although noisy live music sometimes intrudes. Also does decent pub food. No alcohol served from 4–6pm.

Viceroy Bar

MAP P.26, POCKET MAP M13
Four Points Sheraton Hotel, Khalid bin al Waleed Rd. Sharaf DG metro ⓣ 04 397 7444.
This traditional English-style pub is one of the nicest in Bur Dubai, complete with fake oak-beamed ceiling, authentic wooden bar and oodles of comfy leather armchairs.

Deira

North of the Creek lies Deira, the second of the old city's two principal districts, founded in 1841, when settlers from Bur Dubai crossed the Creek to establish a new village here. Deira rapidly overtook its older neighbour in commercial importance and remains notably more built-up and cosmopolitan than Bur Dubai, with a heady ethnic mix of Emiratis, Gulf Arabs, Iranians, Indians, Pakistanis and Somalis thronging its packed streets. Specific tourist attractions are thinner on the ground here than in Bur Dubai, but the district remains the best place in Dubai for aimless wandering, and even the shortest exploration will uncover a kaleidoscopic jumble of cultures, from Indian curry houses and Iranian grocers to Somali shisha cafés and backstreet mosques – not to mention an endless array of shops selling everything from formal black *abbeya* to belly-dancing costumes.

Gold Souk

MAP P.36, POCKET MAP N11

Between Sikkat al Khail Rd and Old Baladiya Rd. Al Ras metro.

Deira's famous **Gold Souk** is usually the first stop for visitors to the district, with over three hundred shops lined up along its wooden-roofed main arcade, their windows packed with a staggering quantity of jewellery – it's been estimated that there are usually around ten tonnes of gold here at any one time. The souk's main attraction is price: the gold available here is among the cheapest in the world, and massive competition keeps prices keen. Though the gold industry in Dubai is carefully regulated, with the daily gold price fixed in all shops citywide, you should always **bargain**. A request for "best price" or "small discount" should yield an immediate discount of around 20–25 percent, although it always pays to shop around. The jewellery on offer ranges from restrained European-style pieces to ornate Arabian creations – the traditional Emirati bracelets, fashioned from solid gold and hung in long lines in shop windows, are particularly appealing.

Heritage House

MAP P.36, POCKET MAP N11

Old Baladiya Rd. Al Ras metro. Closed for renovation at the time of writing.

One of the city's oldest museums, the engaging **Heritage House** offers the most authentic picture of everyday life in old Dubai you'll find anywhere in town. The building (originally constructed in 1890) is a classic example of a traditional Gulf mansion, with rooms arranged around a large sandy courtyard. Each of the rooms is enlivened with exhibits evoking aspects of traditional Emirati life, along with a large cast of elaborately dressed mannequins going about their daily business: drinking coffee, spinning thread, grinding spices and so on, while a couple of waxwork children look incuriously on.

Al Ahmadiya School

MAP P.36, POCKET MAP N11

Old Baladiya Rd, next to the Heritage

House. Al Ras metro. Closed for renovation at the time of writing.

Founded in 1912 by pearl merchant Sheikh Mohammed bin Ahmed bin Dalmouk, the **Al Ahmadiya School** is one of the city's finest surviving examples of traditional Emirati architecture. Al Ahmadiya was the first public school in UAE, and many of the city's leaders studied here – it was also notably egalitarian, with only the sons of wealthy families being expected to pay. Inside, a few modest exhibits explore the educational history of the emirate, with old photos and the inevitable mannequins, including three tiny pupils being instructed by a rather irritable-looking teacher brandishing a wooden cane.

Grand Souk Deira

MAP P.36, POCKET MAP N11

Between Al Ras and Baniyas roads. Al Ras metro.

The extensive covered souk formerly known as Al Souk al Kabeer ("The Big Souk") was once the largest and most important market in Deira. Now rechristened **Grand Souk Deira**, the whole area has been given a major makeover, although most of the shops remain rather dull. Easily the most interesting part of the souk is the diminutive **Spice Souk** (signed "Herbs Market"), perhaps the most atmospheric – and certainly the most fragrant – of the city's many bazaars. Run almost exclusively by Iranian traders, the shops here stock a wide variety of culinary, medicinal and cosmetic products, with tubs of merchandise set out in front of each tiny shopfront, including great piles of frankincense and other exotic commodities.

Museum of the Poet Al Oqaili

MAP P.36, POCKET MAP N11

Off Arsa Court, Grand Souk Deira. Al Ras metro ⓣ 800 33 222, free.

At the back of the Grand Souk is the diminutive Souk Al Arsa, centred on a small courtyard usually full of boxes, trolleys and lounging porters. From here, signs point towards the **Museum of the Poet Al Oqaili**, hidden away in a labyrinthine maze of back alleys. The museum occupies the former house of noted poet Mubarak

The Gold Souk

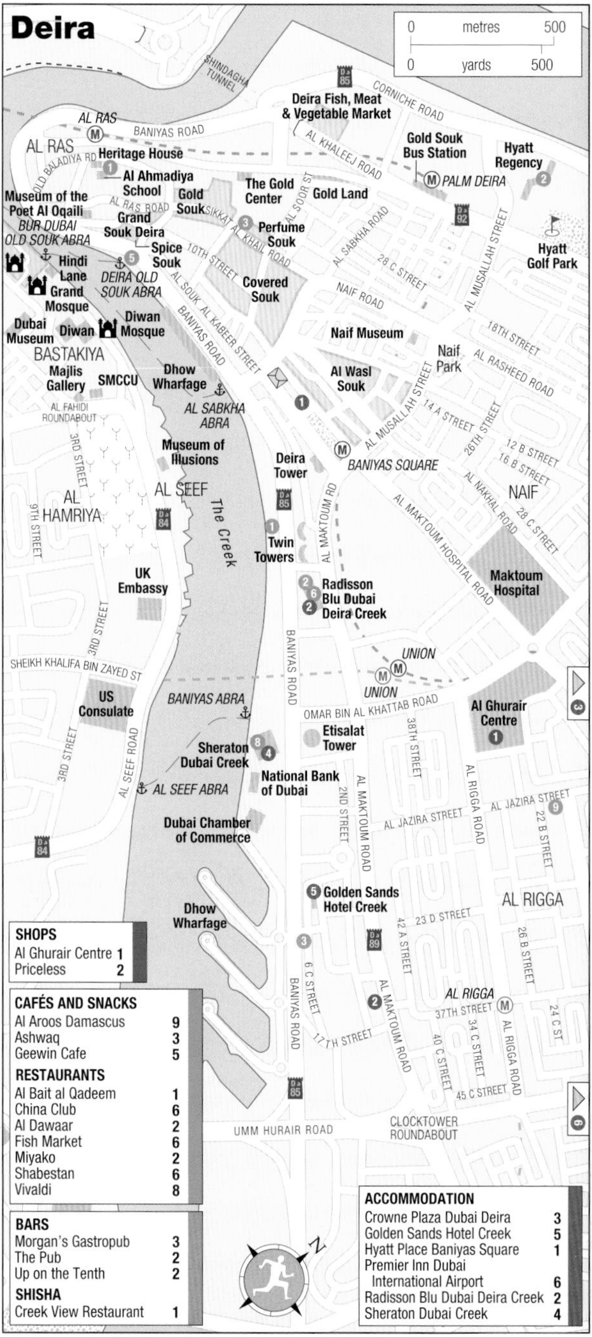

Deira
0 metres 500
0 yards 500
SHINDAGHA TUNNEL
CORNICHE ROAD
Deira Fish, Meat & Vegetable Market
AL RAS
BANIYAS ROAD
AL KHALEEJ ROAD
Gold Souk Bus Station
Hyatt Regency
PALM DEIRA
AL RAS
OLD BALADIYA RD
Heritage House
Al Ahmadiya School
Gold Souk
The Gold Center
Gold Land
AL SOOR ST
Museum of the Poet Al Oqaili
AL RAS ROAD
Grand Souk Deira
SIKKAT AL KHAIL ROAD
Perfume Souk
AL SABKHA ROAD
AL MUSALLAH STREET
Hyatt Golf Park
BUR DUBAI OLD SOUK ABRA
Spice Souk
10TH STREET
28 C STREET
Hindi Lane
DEIRA OLD SOUK ABRA
AL SOUK AL KABEER STREET
Covered Souk
NAIF ROAD
Grand Mosque
Diwan Mosque
BANIYAS ROAD
18TH STREET
Dubai Museum
Diwan
Naif Museum
BASTAKIYA
Naif Park
AL RASHEED ROAD
Majlis Gallery
SMCCU
Dhow Wharfage
Al Wasl Souk
AL SABKHA ABRA
AL MUSALLAH STREET
14 A STREET
AL FAHIDI ROUNDABOUT
26TH STREET
12 B STREET
3RD STREET
Museum of Illusions
BANIYAS SQUARE
16 B STREET
Deira Tower
AL NAKHAL ROAD
NAIF
AL SEEF
AL HAMRIYA
9TH STREET
The Creek
AL MAKTOUM RD
AL MAKTOUM HOSPITAL ROAD
28 C STREET
Twin Towers
UK Embassy
Maktoum Hospital
Radisson Blu Dubai Deira Creek
3RD STREET
UNION
SHEIKH KHALIFA BIN ZAYED ST
UNION
BANIYAS ROAD
US Consulate
BANIYAS ABRA
OMAR BIN AL KHATTAB ROAD
Al Ghurair Centre
Etisalat Tower
Sheraton Dubai Creek
38TH STREET
3RD STREET
AL SEEF ROAD
National Bank of Dubai
AL SEEF ABRA
AL RIGGA ROAD
AL JAZIRA STREET
2ND STREET
AL MAKTOUM ROAD
AL JAZIRA STREET
22 B STREET
Dubai Chamber of Commerce
Golden Sands Hotel Creek
AL RIGGA
Dhow Wharfage
23 D STREET
42 A STREET
26 B STREET
AL RIGGA
6 C STREET
37TH STREET
BANIYAS ROAD
AL MAKTOUM ROAD
34 C STREET
AL RIGGA ROAD
24 C ST
17TH STREET
40 C STREET
45 C STREET
UMM HURAIR ROAD
CLOCKTOWER ROUNDABOUT
SHOPS
Al Ghurair Centre 1
Priceless 2
CAFÉS AND SNACKS
Al Aroos Damascus 9
Ashwaq 3
Geewin Cafe 5
RESTAURANTS
Al Bait al Qadeem 1
China Club 6
Al Dawaar 2
Fish Market 6
Miyako 2
Shabestan 6
Vivaldi 8
BARS
Morgan's Gastropub 3
The Pub 2
Up on the Tenth 2
SHISHA
Creek View Restaurant 1
N
ACCOMMODATION
Crowne Plaza Dubai Deira 3
Golden Sands Hotel Creek 5
Hyatt Place Baniyas Square 1
Premier Inn Dubai International Airport 6
Radisson Blu Dubai Deira Creek 2
Sheraton Dubai Creek 4

Souk Opening Hours

Most of the souk shops are open from around 10am until 10pm, although some may close between 1pm until 4/5pm, and many also close on Friday mornings.

bin Hamad al Manea al Oqaili (1875–1954), who eventually settled in Dubai after an itinerant life in Oman, Abu Dhabi and Bahrain. The house itself (built in 1923) is well worth a look, with two storeys set around a shady central courtyard, embellished with delicately carved stone windows and wooden balustrades – although the exhibits on Al Oqaili himself plumb impressive depths of dullness.

Dhow Wharfage

MAP P.36, POCKET MAP N12

Deira creekside, between Deira Old Souk and Al Sabkha abra stations. Al Ras metro.

The **Dhow Wharfage** offers a fascinating glimpse into the maritime traditions of old Dubai, home to dozens of beautiful wooden dhows which berth here to load and unload cargo – hence the great tarpaulin-covered mounds of merchandise lying stacked up along the waterfront. The dhows themselves range in size from the fairly modest vessels employed for short hops up and down the coast to the large ocean-going craft used to transport goods around the Gulf and over to Iran, and even as far afield as Somalia, Pakistan and India. Virtually all of them fly the UAE flag, although they're generally manned by foreign crews who live on board.

Perfume Souk

MAP P.36, POCKET MAP 011

Sikkat al Khail Rd, immediately east of the Gold Souk. Al Ras metro.

Deira's **Perfume Souk** stretches along the western end of Sikkat al Khail Road, and also spills over into Al Soor and Souk Deira streets. Most of the shops here sell a mix of international brands (not necessarily genuine) along with the much heavier and more flowery oil-based *attar* perfumes favoured by local ladies. At many places you can also create your own scents, mixing and matching from the contents of the big bottles lined up behind the counter before taking them away in chintzy little cut-glass containers, many of which are collectibles.

Covered Souk

MAP P.36, POCKET MAP 011

Between Souk Deira St and Al Sabkha Rd.

Deira's sprawling **Covered Souk** (a misnomer, since it isn't) comprises a rather indeterminate area of small shops arranged around the maze of narrow, pedestrianized alleyways which run south from Sikkat al Khail Road down towards the Creek. Most of the shops here are Indian-run, selling colourful, low-grade cloth for women's clothes, along with large quantities of mass-

Dhow Wharfage

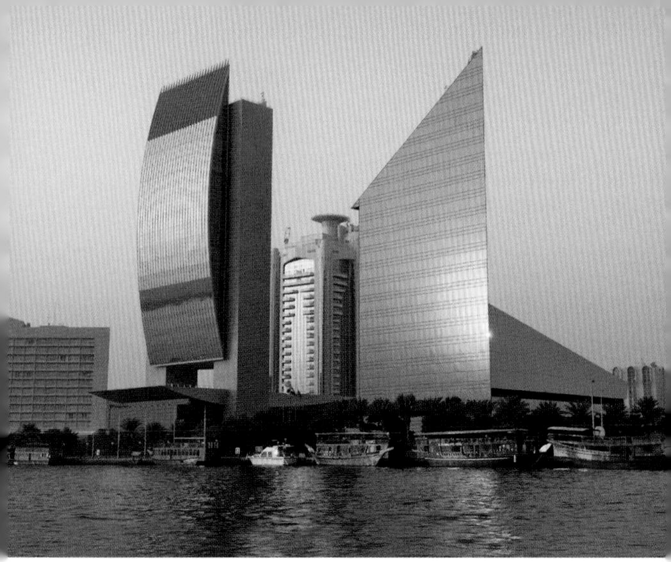

The National Bank of Dubai

produced plastic toys and cheap household goods. It's all rather down-at-heel, but makes for an interesting stroll, especially in the area at the back of the Al Sabkha bus station, the densest and busiest part of the bazaar, particularly after dark – expect to get lost at least once. The souk then continues, more or less unabated, on the far side of Al Sabkha Road, where it's known variously as the **Naif Souk** and **Al Wasl Souk**, before reaching Al Musallah Street.

Naif Museum

MAP P.36, POCKET MAP O2
Naif Police Station, Naif Fort, Sikkat al Khail Rd. Baniyas Square metro ⓘ 800 33 222, free.
Celebrating Dubai's formidable reputation for law and order, the modest **Naif Museum** lies tucked away in a corner of the imposing Naif Fort (originally built in 1939 but restored to death in 1997). It's actually a lot less tedious than you might fear, with mildly interesting exhibits on the history of law enforcement in the emirate from the foundation of the police force in 1956 (with just six officers under a British captain) up to the present day. Exhibits include assorted old weapons and uniforms, various old photos and a trio of short films including some interesting historical footage.

The National Bank of Dubai and around

MAP P.36, POCKET MAP N3
Off Baniyas Rd immediately south of the Sheraton Dubai Creek Hotel. Union metro.
Next to the Creek in the southern part of Deira you'll find several of Dubai's original modernist landmarks. Pride of place goes to the **National Bank of Dubai** building (1998), its Creek-facing side covered by an enormous, curved sheet of highly polished glass, modelled on the sail of a traditional dhow. Next to the bank sits the shorter and squatter **Dubai Chamber of Commerce** (1995), an austerely minimalist glass-clad structure which seems to have been designed using nothing but triangles, while nearby on Omar bin al Khattab Road stands the **Etisalat Tower** (1986), instantly recognizable thanks to the enormous golf ball on its roof.

Shops

Al Ghurair Centre

MAP P.36, POCKET MAP O3
Al Rigga Rd, alghuraircentre.com; Union metro.
One of Dubai's oldest malls (complete with landmark postmodern windtowers, illuminated in eye-catching blues after dark) and now second only to BurJuman as the old city's best one-stop shopping destination with a wide range of shops spread over three floors (including lots of places selling local perfumes, fabrics and flouncy dresses), while the top-floor food court is a convenient place to pick up a drink or quick bite to eat.

Priceless

MAP P.36, POCKET MAP O4
Al Maktoum Rd, near Deira Clock Tower. Al Rigga metro 04 221 5444.
Worth the schlep for the excellent spread of top designer menswear and ladieswear – Armani, Yves Saint-Laurent, Gucci and the like – all sold at big discounts; two-thirds off label prices is standard.

Cafés and snacks

Al Aroos Damascus

MAP P.36, POCKET MAP O3
Al Muraqqabat Rd. Al Rigga metro, aroosdamascus.com.
One of a number of lively local Middle Eastern restaurants along Al Muraqqabat Road – Dubai's "Little Iraq" – and parallel Al Rigga Road. All the usual Lebanese mezze and grills are on offer – well cooked, reasonably priced and served in huge portions. Dh

Ashwaq

MAP P.36, POCKET MAP O11
Perfume Souk, Sikkat al Khail Rd. Al Ras metro 04 226 1164.
Close to the entrance to the bustling Gold Souk, this is one of the busiest and best of Deira's various shwarma stands, with melt-in-the-mouth shwarma sandwiches and big fruit juices. Dh

Geewin Cafe

MAP P.26, POCKET MAP N2
Baniyas Rd.
Cool off with a scoop of camel-milk ice cream (25dh) at this tiny waterfront kiosk next to the Deira Old Souk abra station, with traditional flavours including saffron and almonds with dates. Dh

Restaurants

Al Bait al Qadeem

MAP P.36, POCKET MAP N2
Old Baladiya Rd. Al Ras metro, albaitalqadeem.com.
In a traditional building right next to the Heritage House, with an attractive courtyard at the back and a pretty dining room. Food (mains 40–70dh) features well-prepared and reasonably-priced regional dishes along with more mainstream Lebanese-style kebabs. DhDh

China Club

MAP P.36, POCKET MAP O13
Radisson Blu Dubai Deira Creek Hotel, Baniyas Rd. Union metro 04 205 7033.
The best Chinese restaurant in central Dubai, offering a regular "Yum Cha" buffets plus a good range of à la carte choices, including the restaurant's signature *dim sum* and Peking duck. DhDhDh

Al Dawaar

MAP P.36, POCKET MAP O1
Hyatt Regency Hotel, Corniche Rd. Gold Souq metro 04 209 6912.
Dubai's only revolving restaurant, offering superlative city views. Food is buffet only (249dh at lunch; 229dh at dinner, excluding drinks), featuring a mix of Arabian, Mediterranean and Japanese cuisines – not the city's greatest culinary experience, but a decent

accompaniment to the head-turning vistas outside. DhDhDh

Fish Market

MAP P.36, POCKET MAP O13
Radisson Blu Hotel, Baniyas Rd. Union metro ⓜ 04 222 7171.

Given its location right on the Arabian Gulf there's a surprising lack of seafood restaurants in Dubai, a gap which the bright and breezy Fish Market restaurant has been faithfully plugging ever since first opening its doors way back in 1989. Select what you fancy from the huge selection of freshly landed fish and seafood at the restaurant's "market" after which resident chefs which prepare it in a style of your choice. DhDhDh

Miyako

MAP P.36, POCKET MAP O1
Hyatt Regency Hotel, Corniche Rd. Gold Souq metro ⓜ 04 209 6912.

Another long-running stalwart of the old city's international dining scene. Miyako is generally rated one of the best Japanese restaurants anywhere in Dubai and refreshingly affordable given the quality with a range of noodles, teppanyaki, sushi and maki, plus great bento boxes. A good option at lunch too, when you can grab a tasty bowl of soba, ramen or udon for just 60–75dh. lunch DhDh, dinner DhDhDh

Shabestan

MAP P.36, POCKET MAP O13
Radisson Blu Dubai Deira Creek Hotel,

Al Aroos Damascus

Baniyas Rd. Union metro
04 205 7033.

This sedate, upmarket Iranian restaurant retains a loyal following among Emiratis and expat Iranians thanks to its huge *chelo* kebabs, fish stews and other Persian specialities like *baghalah polo* (slow-cooked lamb) and *zereshk polo* (baked chicken with wild berries). DhDhDhDh

Vivaldi

MAP P.36, POCKET MAP N3
Sheraton Dubai Creek Hotel, Baniyas Rd. Union metro, vivaldidubai.com.

Long-running Italian now sporting stylish modern decor to go with its sweeping Creek views. The menu features artful modern Italian mains alongside a good and reasonably priced selection of pasta and pizza. DhDh

Bars

Morgan's Gastropub

MAP P.36, POCKET MAP N4
Al Bandar Rotana Hotel, Baniyas Rd. Union metro 04 704 2331.

Swanky modern pub-cum-restaurant serving up a wide range of tipples including around ten different draught beers (from 40dh), plus a reasonable wine list and cocktail selection, with significant saving during the daily happy hour (noon–6pm) when you can get cocktails, wine or draught beers for a steal by Dubai standards. There's also above-average international pub food serving everything from butter chicken and wasabi prawns to tacos and burgers.

The Pub

MAP P.36, POCKET MAP 013
Radisson Blu Dubai Deira Creek Hotel, Baniyas Rd. Union metro 04 205 7033.

Spacious and usually fairly peaceful English-style pub, complete with the usual fake wooden bar and lots of TVs screening global sports.

Issimo Bar

Happy hour (20 percent discounts) daily 6–9pm.

Up on the Tenth

MAP P.36, POCKET MAP 013
10th floor, Radisson Blu Dubai Deira Creek Hotel, Baniyas Rd. Union metro 04 222 7171.

One of Dubai's best-kept secrets, offering just about the best Creek views to be had in the city centre. Arrive early, grab a window seat and watch the city light up. A jazz singer and pianist perform most nights from 10pm.

Shisha

Creek View Restaurant

MAP P.36, POCKET MAP 013
Baniyas Rd. Baniyas Square metro, www.creekviewdubai.net.

This convivial open-air café scores highly for its breezy creekside location and lively late-night atmosphere. It's a good place for an after-dinner smoke (with thirteen types of shisha) and coffee, although the food (mainly mezze and kebabs) is only so-so. No alcohol.

The inner suburbs

Fringing the southern and eastern edges of the city centre – and separating it from the more modern areas beyond – is a necklace of low-key suburbs: Garhoud, Oud Metha, Karama and Satwa. South of Deira, workaday Garhoud is home to the Dubai Creek Golf Club, with its famously futuristic clubhouse, and the adjacent yacht club, where you'll find a string of attractive waterside restaurants alongside the lovely *Park Hyatt* hotel. Directly over the Creek, Oud Metha is home to the quirky Wafi complex and the lavish Khan Murjan Souk, while west of here the enjoyably downmarket suburbs of Karama and Satwa are both interesting places to get off the tourist trail and see something of local life among the city's Indian and Filipino expats, with plenty of cheap curry houses and shops selling designer fakes, while nearby is one of the city's newest landmarks, the wonderfully outlandish Dubai Frame.

Garhoud

MAP P.44, POCKET MAP N5–O7
Deira City Centre metro.

Covering the area between the airport and the Creek, the suburb of **Garhoud** is an interesting mishmash of up- and downmarket attractions. The **Deira City Centre** mall (see page 47) is the main draw for locals, while on the far side of Baniyas Road lies the **Dubai Creek Golf Club**, an impressive swathe of lush fairways centred on the quirky clubhouse, with its uniquely spiky white roofline echoing the shape of a dhow's sails and masts. Close by you'll find the **Dubai Creek Yacht Club**, occupying a full-sized replica of a ship's bridge, with dozens of beautiful yachts moored alongside and a cluster of good restaurants lining the waterfront. Next door sits the beguiling **Park Hyatt** hotel, its serene white Moroccan-style buildings, topped with vivid blue-tiled domes, adding a further touch of style to the creekside hereabouts.

Wafi and Khan Murjan Souk

MAP P.44, POCKET MAP L6
Junction of Oud Metha and Sheikh Rashid roads. Dubai Healthcare City metro ⓣ 04 324 4555, ⓦ wafi.com. Daily 10am–10pm (Thurs & Fri until midnight).

The wacky Egyptian-themed **Wafi** complex is a little slice of Vegas in Dubai, dotted with obelisks, pharaonic statues, random hieroglyphs and assorted miniature pyramids. The mall is home to myriad boutiques and restaurants (see pages 47 and 48). The Egyptian theme is continued in the opulent **Raffles** hotel next door, built in the form of a vast pyramid, its summit capped with glass – particularly spectacular when lit up after dark.

Attached to Wafi is the lavish **Khan Murjan Souk**, one of Dubai's finest "traditional" developments, allegedly modelled after the fabled fourteenth-century Khan Murjan Souk in Baghdad, with around 125 shops selling all manner of traditional wares and a

Shopping for fakes

Despite occasional government clampdowns, Dubai's vibrant trade in **counterfeit goods** (bags, watches, sunglasses, pens, DVDs and so on) is still going strong. Spend any amount of time in Karama Souk, the Gold Souk or around Al Fahidi Street in Bur Dubai and you'll be repeatedly importuned with offers of "cheap copy watches" or "copy bags", as the souks' enthusiastic touts euphemistically describe them. Many fakes are still relatively expensive – you're unlikely to find bigger-ticket items for much under $75, and plenty of items cost double that, although they'll still be a lot cheaper than the real thing. Fakes may look convincing, but longevity varies considerably; some items can fall to pieces within a fortnight, and it's essential to check quality carefully – particularly stitching and zips – and be prepared to shop around and bargain like crazy.

lovely outdoor restaurant (see page 48). It's a great (albeit pricey) place to shop, while the faux-Arabian decor is impressively done, with lavish detailing ranging from intricately carved wooden balconies to enormous Moroccan lanterns and colourful tilework.

AYA

MAP P.44, POCKET MAP L6
Wafi. Dubai Healthcare City metro ⓣ 04 542 0300, ⓦ www.aya-universe.com. Daily 10am–10pm (Thurs & Fri until midnight). 125dh (or 99dh if book online in advance).

Wafi is also where you'll find the futuristic new AYA attraction – a kind of immersive visual extravanga built for the Instagram age. Inside, the 12 elaborately mirrored, sense-twisting spaces are filled with swirling visual effects which cover every available surface – submarine corals, kaleidoscopic fractals, exploding galaxies. Endlessly refracted images create the illusion of vast plains covered in luminous flowers or endless starry skies, while solid floors transform into whorls of light and drops of water fall upwards. Just be careful not to walk into any walls.

Creek Park

MAP P.44, POCKET MAP M5–7
Riyadh Rd. Dubai Healthcare City or Oud

Wafi's Egyptian-inspired facade

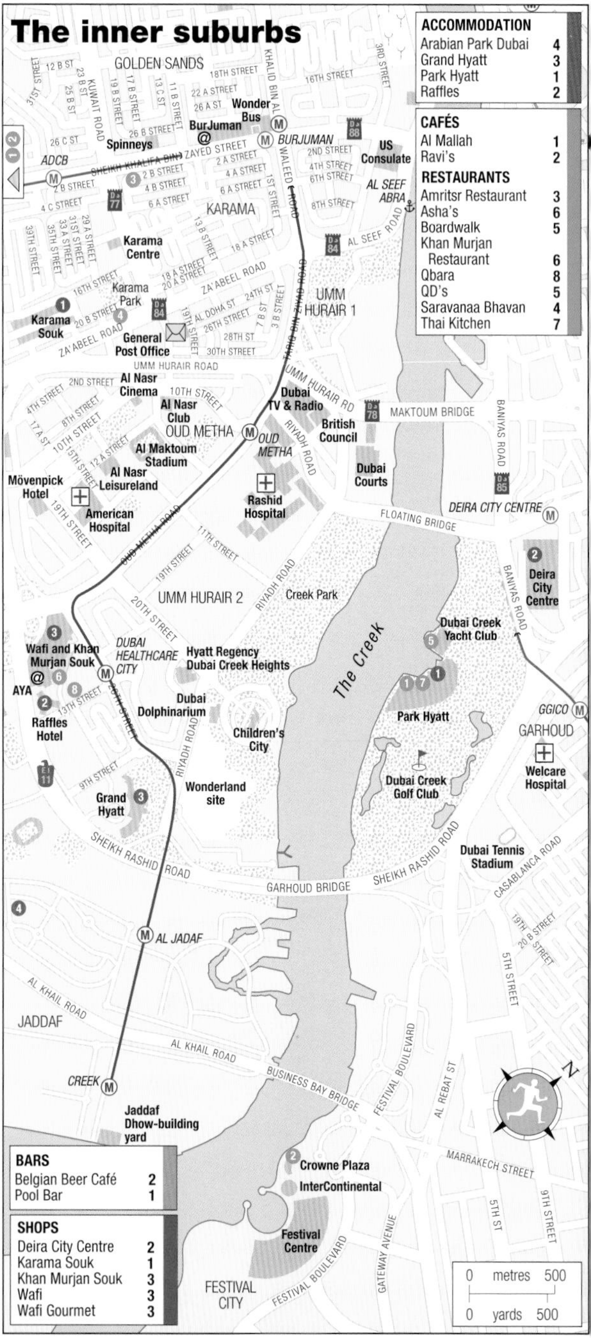
The inner suburbs
ACCOMMODATION
Arabian Park Dubai 4
Grand Hyatt 3
Park Hyatt 1
Raffles 2
CAFÉS
Al Mallah 1
Ravi's 2
RESTAURANTS
Amritsr Restaurant 3
Asha's 6
Boardwalk 5
Khan Murjan Restaurant 6
Qbara 8
QD's 5
Saravanaa Bhavan 4
Thai Kitchen 7
BARS
Belgian Beer Café 2
Pool Bar 1
SHOPS
Deira City Centre 2
Karama Souk 1
Khan Murjan Souk 3
Wafi 3
Wafi Gourmet 3
GOLDEN SANDS
KARAMA
BurJuman
Wonder Bus
BURJUMAN
Spinneys
ADCB
US Consulate
AL SEEF ABRA
Karama Centre
Karama Park
Karama Souk
General Post Office
UMM HURAIR 1
Al Nasr Cinema
Al Nasr Club
OUD METHA
Dubai TV & Radio
British Council
MAKTOUM BRIDGE
Al Maktoum Stadium
Al Nasr Leisureland
Mövenpick Hotel
American Hospital
Rashid Hospital
Dubai Courts
DEIRA CITY CENTRE
FLOATING BRIDGE
Deira City Centre
UMM HURAIR 2
Creek Park
The Creek
Dubai Creek Yacht Club
Wafi and Khan Murjan Souk
DUBAI HEALTHCARE CITY
Hyatt Regency Dubai Creek Heights
AYA
Raffles Hotel
Dubai Dolphinarium
Children's City
Park Hyatt
GGICO
GARHOUD
Welcare Hospital
Wonderland site
Grand Hyatt
Dubai Creek Golf Club
Dubai Tennis Stadium
SHEIKH RASHID ROAD
GARHOUD BRIDGE
AL JADAF
AL KHAIL ROAD
JADDAF
BUSINESS BAY BRIDGE
CREEK
Jaddaf Dhow-building yard
Crowne Plaza
InterContinental
Festival Centre
FESTIVAL CITY
FESTIVAL BOULEVARD
GATEWAY AVENUE
MARRAKECH STREET
CASABLANCA ROAD
AL REBAT ST
KHALID BIN AL WALEED ROAD
TARIQ BIN ZIYAD ROAD
OUD METHA ROAD
RIYADH ROAD
ZA'ABEEL ROAD
UMM HURAIR ROAD
BANIYAS ROAD
AL SEEF ROAD
SHEIKH KHALIFA BIN ZAYED STREET
KUWAIT ROAD
0 metres 500
0 yards 500

Metha metros. Daily 8am–10pm. 5dh.
Flanking the Creek, the expansive **Creek Park** serves as one of congested central Dubai's major lungs and is a pleasant place for an idle ramble, with good views over the Creek towards the golf and yacht clubs –nicest towards dusk, when the temperature falls and the place fills up a bit. It's particularly good for kids, with plenty of playgrounds and the fun **Children's City** (see page 117).

Karama

MAP P.44, POCKET MAP L3–4
Karama metro.
Karama is the classic Dubai inner-city suburb, home to some of the legions of Indian, Pakistani and Filipino expat workers who supply so much of the city's labour. The district is centred on **Kuwait Street** and the bustling little **Karama Centre**, with colourful shops selling *shalwar kameez* and Indian-style jewellery. At the end of Kuwait Street lies the lively **Karama Park**, surrounded by cheap and cheery Indian restaurants. South of here is the district's main tourist attraction, the **Karama Souk**, with hundreds of small shops stuffed full of fake designer clothes, watches, glasses, DVDs and other items.

Dubai Frame

POCKET MAP K4
Gate 4, Zabeel Park. Al Jafiliya metro. ⓣ800 900, ⓦdubaiframe.ae; daily 9am–9pm. 50dh.
On the south side of Karama, the wonderfully weird **Dubai Frame** can be regarded either a spectacularly large picture frame or a very oddly shaped building – the brainchild of Mexican architect Fernando Donis, who stated that Dubai had enough landmarks and already and that rather than adding another he would create a frame large enough to capture the entire city. Standing over 150m (492ft), an elevator carries visitors to the observation platform at the top of the structure, offering peerless views of both old and new cities, while a museum at the base showcases Dubai's history and hints at future developments.

Satwa

POCKET MAP H2–J2
The unpretentious district of **Satwa** is the most southerly of Dubai's predominantly low-rise, low-income inner suburbs before you reach the giant skyscrapers of Sheikh Zayed Road. It's also one of the few places in Dubai where the city's different ethnic groups really rub shoulders, reflected in an unusually eclectic selection of places to eat, from cheap-and-cheerful curry houses to Lebanese shwarma cafés and Western fast-food joints.

At the centre of the district lies **Satwa Roundabout**. The streets south of here are mainly occupied by Indian and Pakistani shops and cafés, including the well-known *Ravi's* restaurant (see page 48). West from the roundabout stretches

The Dubai Frame

the tree-lined **2 December Street** (formerly Al Diyafah Street), one of the nicest in Dubai – and one of the few outside the city centre boasting any real street life. It's lined with dozens of casual eateries and offers an interesting insight into a more down to earth side of life that you won't come across in Dubai too often.

Festival City

MAP P.44, POCKET MAP M9

Festival Boulevard ⓦ dubaifestivalcity.com.

Festival City is one of Dubai's newer purpose-built neighbourhoods – a self-contained city within a city, complete with the requisite offices, golf course, marina, shopping mall and swanky hotels. Centrepiece of the development is the bright, modern **Festival Centre** shopping mall: relatively small beer compared to other malls around the city, although there are fine views from the waterfront promenade outside across the water to the dhow-building yards at Jaddaf and the long line of skyscrapers beyond. Reaching the area is easiest by taxi, although there's also a useful abra service connecting it with Creek metro station (daily 8am–11.30pm; 2dh)

Ras al Khor Wildlife Sanctuary

POCKET MAP Q8

Ras al Khor/Oud Metha roads ⓣ 800 900, ⓦ www.dm.gov.ae/dubai-protected-areas. Oct–March: daily 7.30am–5.30pm; April–Sept: daily 6am–6pm, Fri 2–6pm. Free.

Some 8km inland, the Dubai Creek widens into the impressive **Ras al Khor** ("Head of the Creek"), forming an extensive inland lagoon dotted with mangroves and surrounded by intertidal salt and mud flats – a unique area of unspoilt nature close to the city centre. The western end of the lagoon now connects directly with the recently opened Dubai Water Canal (see page 62), forming a single unbroken loop of water stretching from the old city to Jumeirah. A trip along the entire length of the newly connected waterways would undoubtedly be Dubai's ultimate boat excursion, although sadly there are no scheduled services at present.

The southern end of the lagoon is home to the low-key **Ras al Khor Wildlife Sanctuary**, best known for its aquatic birdlife. The sanctuary is an important stopover on winter migratory routes from East Africa to West Asia and almost seventy different species have been spotted here. It's best known for the colourful flocks of bright pink flamingoes which nest here – one of Dubai's most surreal sights when seen perched against the smoggy outlines of the city skyscrapers beyond. You can birdwatch for free from one of two **hides** on its edge, while visits inside the reserve can be booked online through the website. Signage for the hides is minimal and you'll need a car to reach them, but don't expect taxi drivers to know where they are.

Meydan

POCKET MAP C9

Meydan Rd (take exit 7 off the E66 Al Ain Rd, or exit 20 off Al Khail Rd (E44), around 4km south of Ras al Khor ⓦ meydan.ae.

The vast **Meydan** complex provides conclusive proof of the ruling Maktoum family's passion – bordering on obsession – for all things equine. Sheikh Mohammed's love of horses runs deep. He is said as a youth to have been able to tame wild horses considered unrideable by others and later went on to found Godolphin, one of the world's most successful racing stables (although its reputation was seriously tarnished by a doping scandal in 2013). Centrepiece of the complex is the superb **Meydan racecourse**, which is the venue for the **Dubai World Cup**, the world's richest horse race with a massive $12 million in prize money.

Shops

Deira City Centre

MAP P.44, POCKET MAP O5
Garhoud. Deira City Centre metro
Ⓦ citycentredeira.com. Daily 10am–10pm (Thurs–Sat until midnight).

This big old mall remains one of the most popular in the city, with 340-plus outlets covering the whole retail spectrum, including oodles of cut-price electronics alongside fashion, jewellery and perfumes in all price ranges. Ali Al Jazeeri (on the top floor) is a great place to try if you fancy kitting yourself out in a set of haute-couture Emirati-style robes plus headdress.

Karama Souk

MAP P.44, POCKET MAP L4
Karama. ADCB metro. Most shops open daily 10am–10pm.

The best place to find fake designer gear, with dozens of shops stacked full of imitation designer clothing and bags and "genuine fake watches". There are also a few low-grade souvenir shops dotted around the souk selling kitsch classics like mosque alarm clocks and miniature Burj al Arabs moulded in glass.

Khan Murjan Souk

MAP P.44, POCKET MAP L6
Wafi, Oud Metha. Dubai Healthcare City metro Ⓦ wafi.com/souk. Daily 10am–10pm (Fri & Sat until midnight).

The hundred-plus stores in this superb replica souk (see page 42) comprise the city's best and most upmarket array of traditional crafts shops, selling just about every kind of Arabian gewgaw, artefact and antique you can think of.

Wafi

MAP P.44, POCKET MAP L6
Oud Metha. Dubai Healthcare City metro Ⓦ wafi.com. Daily 10am–10pm (Thurs & Fri until midnight).

This zany Egyptian-themed mall makes for a pleasantly superior shopping experience, with branches of Wafi Gourmet (see below), Emad Carpets (see opposite) and some good fashion boutiques, including local ladieswear favourite Ginger & Lace.

Karama Souk

Wafi Gourmet

MAP P.44, POCKET MAP L6
Wafi, Oud Metha. Dubai Healthcare City metro Ⓣ 04 327 9940, Ⓦ wafigourmet.com. Daily 10am–10pm (Thurs & Fri until midnight).

The ultimate Dubai deli, piled high with tempting Middle Eastern items, including big buckets of olives, nuts, spices and dried fruits, and trays of date rolls, baklava and fine chocolates, plus an attached café. Other branches in Dubai Mall and Jumeirah.

Cafés

Al Mallah

MAP P.44, POCKET MAP J2
Al Diyafah St. Max metro Ⓣ 04 398 4723, Ⓦ www.almallahuae.com. Daily 7am–2.30am.

A classic slice of Satwa nightlife, this no-frills Lebanese café churns out good shwarmas, grills and other Middle Eastern food at bargain prices to a lively local crowd; the pavement terrace is a great place to people-watch. Dh

Ravi's

MAP P.44, POCKET MAP J2
Satwa Rd, just south of Satwa Roundabout. Al Jafiliya metro. 04 331 5353. Daily 5am–2am.
This famous little Pakistani café, located between the copycat *Ravi Palace* and *Rawi Palace* restaurants, attracts a loyal local and expat clientele thanks to its tasty and inexpensive array of subcontinental standards. There's seating inside, but it's more fun (despite the traffic) to sit out on the pavement and watch the street life of Satwa drift by. Dh

Restaurants

Amritsr Restaurant

MAP P.44. POCKET MAP L3
Al Attar Centre. ADCB metro 04 327 8622, amritsruae.com. Daily 6pm–1am.

Waterside seats at Boardwalk

One of the best of the innumerable Indian and Filipino budget restaurants which fill the streets of Karama, serving up quality, authentic Punjabi cuisine with a wide-ranging selection of both meat and veg options, plus delectable *kulcha* (miniature naan breads). Dh

Asha's

MAP P.44, POCKET MAP L6
Wafi, Oud Metha. Dubai Healthcare City metro 04 324 4100, ashasrestaurants.com. Daily 12.30–3.30pm & 7pm–midnight.
Named after legendary Bollywood chanteuse Asha Bhosle, with sleek modern orange decor and an interesting menu featuring traditional North Indian classics alongside recipes from Bhosle's own family cookbook. Mains DhDhDh

Boardwalk

MAP P.44, POCKET MAP N6
Dubai Creek Yacht Club, Garhoud. Deira City Centre metro 04 295 6000, dubaigolf.com/dine. Daily noon–midnight.
Sleek modern restaurant on the yacht club's Creekside boardwalk, with stunning city views and a mainly Italian and Mediterranean-style menu featuring lots of seafood and pizza, plus tasty antipasti. DhDhDh

Khan Murjan Restaurant

MAP P.44, POCKET MAP L6
Souk Khan Murjan, Wafi, Oud Metha. Dubai Healthcare City metro 04 327 9795. Daily 10am–1am.
The centrepiece of the spectacular Souk Khan Murjan, this beautiful courtyard restaurant has proved a big hit with the city's Emiratis and expat Arabs, thanks to the traditional atmosphere and unusually wide-ranging menu, featuring tempting selections from assorted Middle Eastern cuisines. DhDhDh

Qbara

MAP P.44. POCKET MAP L6
Al Razi St (next to Raffles hotel). Dubai

Healthcare City metro Ⓣ 04 709 2500, Ⓦ qbara.ae. Daily 6pm–1am.

Gorgeously romantic restaurant-cum-lounge-bar – it feels like being inside a rather sexy planetarium. Food is fine dining with a pronounced Arabian twist, featuring inventive and mouthwatering mezze and mains, plus grills and Australian steaks. DhDhDhDh

QD's

MAP P.44, POCKET MAP N6
Dubai Creek Yacht Club, Garhoud. Deira City Centre metro Ⓣ 04 295 6000, Ⓦ dubaigolf.com/dine. Daily 5pm–2am, Thurs, Fri & Sat till 3am.

Fun and good-value restaurant-cum-bar-cum-shisha-café in a superb location on a large open-air terrace overlooking the Creek. The international menu features lots of pizzas and Lebanese kebabs, and there's also a big selection of shisha and a well-stocked bar. DhDh

Saravanaa Bhavan

MAP P.44, POCKET MAP L4
Karama Park. ADCB metro Ⓦ uae.saravanabhavan.com. Daily 8am–11pm.

Overlooking Karama Park, this is one of half a dozen branches of the famous Saravanaa Bhavan Indian restaurant chain in Dubai. Décor is functional, but the pure-veg food is reliably excellent and about as cheap as you'll find anywhere in the city, with a vast selection of dishes to choose from. Dh

Thai Kitchen

MAP P.44, POCKET MAP N6
Park Hyatt Hotel, Garhoud. Deira City Centre metro Ⓣ 04 602 1814. Daily 6pm–midnight.

Occupying part of the *Park Hyatt*'s lovely creekside terrace, this very smooth restaurant serves up a good range of classic Thai dishes, well prepared and with plenty of flavour and spice – or try one of the street-food style sharing menus. DhDhDh

Ravi's

Bars

Belgian Beer Café

MAP P.44, POCKET MAP M9
Crowne Plaza Hotel, Festival City Ⓣ 04 701 1127, Ⓦ facebook.com/belgianbeercafedubai. Daily noon–2am (Fri & Sat until 3am).

Convivial Belgian-style pub-cum-restaurant, with an eye-catching traditional wooden interior, an excellent range of speciality beers on tap or by the bottle (including draught Hoegaarden, Leffe and Belle-Vue Kriek) and good traditional Flemish cooking.

Pool Bar

MAP P.44, POCKET MAP N6
Park Hyatt Dubai, Garhoud Ⓣ 04 602 1814. Daily 9am–10pm.

Order your drinks while you cool off in the pool at this swim-up bar. They also serve finger food and snacks, but nothing that would make you stay out of the water for too long.

Sheikh Zayed Road and Downtown Dubai

Around 5km (3 miles) south of the Creek, the upwardly mobile suburbs of southern Dubai begin in spectacular style with the massed skyscrapers of Sheikh Zayed Road and the huge Downtown Dubai development: an extraordinary sequence of neck-cricking high-rises which march south from the landmark Emirates Towers to the cloud-capped Burj Khalifa, the world's tallest building. This is the modern city at its most futuristic and flamboyant, and perhaps the defining example of Dubai's insatiable desire to offer more luxury, more glitz and more retail opportunities than the competition, with a string of record-breaking attractions which now include not just the world's tallest building but also its largest mall, tallest hotel and biggest fountain.

Emirates Towers

MAP P.52, POCKET MAP G4
Sheikh Zayed Rd. Emirates Towers metro
Ⓦ jumeirah.com/en/stay/dubai/jumeirah-emirates-towers.

Opened in 2000, the soaring **Emirates Towers** remain one of modern Dubai's most iconic symbols, despite increasing competition from newer and even more massive landmarks. The larger office tower (355m/1099ft) was the tallest building in the Middle East and tenth highest in the world when it was completed, though now it just scrapes into the top ten tallest buildings in the city.

Emirates Towers

Museum of the Future

MAP P.52, POCKET MAP H4
Sheikh Zayed Rd. Emirates Towers metro
Ⓣ 04 800 2071, Ⓦ museumofthefuture.ae/en; Daily 10am–9.30pm. 149dh.

Opened in 2022, the funky **Museum of the Future** has already established itself as one of Dubai's most brilliantly original and instantly recognizable landmarks. The gleaming ovoid structure has been described variously as either a giant eye or a squashed doughnut (or, more technically, as a "torus with an elliptical void"), while the elaborate swirls of Arabian calligraphy (they're actually windows) which cover the exterior simultaneously reference the region's cultural roots. Inside, displays evoke the world as it might become by the year 2071, with displays ranging from a digitially simulated rainforest through to a trip aboard the imaginary space station *OSS Hope*.

Dubai International Financial Centre

MAP P.52, POCKET MAP G4
Between Sheikh Zayed Rd and 312 Rd. Emirates Towers metro Ⓦ difc.ae.

The **Dubai International Financial Centre (DIFC)** is the city's financial hub and home to myriad banks, investment companies and other enterprises. The DIFC's northern end is marked by **The Gate**, a striking building looking like a kind of postmodern Arc de Triomphe-cum-office block. The Gate is surrounded on three sides by further buildings linked by "The Balcony", an attractive raised terrace lined with assorted cafés and shops. Off on the east side of the complex is the **Gate Village**, now one of the focal points of Dubai's burgeoning visual arts scene, with virtually every building occupied by assorted galleries.

Dubai World Trade Centre

MAP P.52, POCKET MAP J4
Sheikh Zayed Rd, by Trade Centre Roundabout. World Trade Centre metro Ⓦ dwtc.com.

On the north side of the sprawling **Dubai International Convention and Exhibition Centre** rises the venerable old **Dubai World Trade Centre** tower, Dubai's first skyscraper. Commissioned in 1979 by the visionary Sheikh Rashid, then ruler of Dubai, this 39-storey edifice was widely regarded as a massive white elephant when it was first built, standing as it did in the middle of what was then empty desert far from the old city centre. Contrary to expectations it proved an enormous success, serving as an important anchor for future development along the strip and fully justifying Sheikh Rashid's far-sighted ambition.

Al Yaqoub Tower

Along Sheikh Zayed Road

MAP P.52, POCKET MAP F4–H4.

A more or less unbroken line of high-rises lines Sheikh Zayed Road south of the Emirates Towers. Heading down the strip brings you almost immediately to the daft **Al Yaqoub Tower**: effectively a postmodern replica of London's Big Ben, although at 330m (1083ft) it's well over three times the height of the 96m-tall (315ft) UK original.

Continuing down the road brings you to the slender **Gevora Hotel**, finished in 2017 and, at 356m (1168ft), officially the world's tallest hotel, while just two doors down is the graceful **Rose Rayhaan hotel** (333m/1093ft), which held the same record itself from 2007 to 2012. Slightly further south the strip reaches a suitably dramatic end with the iconic **Dusit Thani** hotel, a towering glass-and-metal edifice inspired by the traditional Thai *wai*, a prayer-like gesture of welcome, though it looks more like a huge upended tuning fork thrust into the ground.

Burj Khalifa

MAP P.52, POCKET MAP E4
Sheikh Mohammed bin Rashid Blvd (Emaar

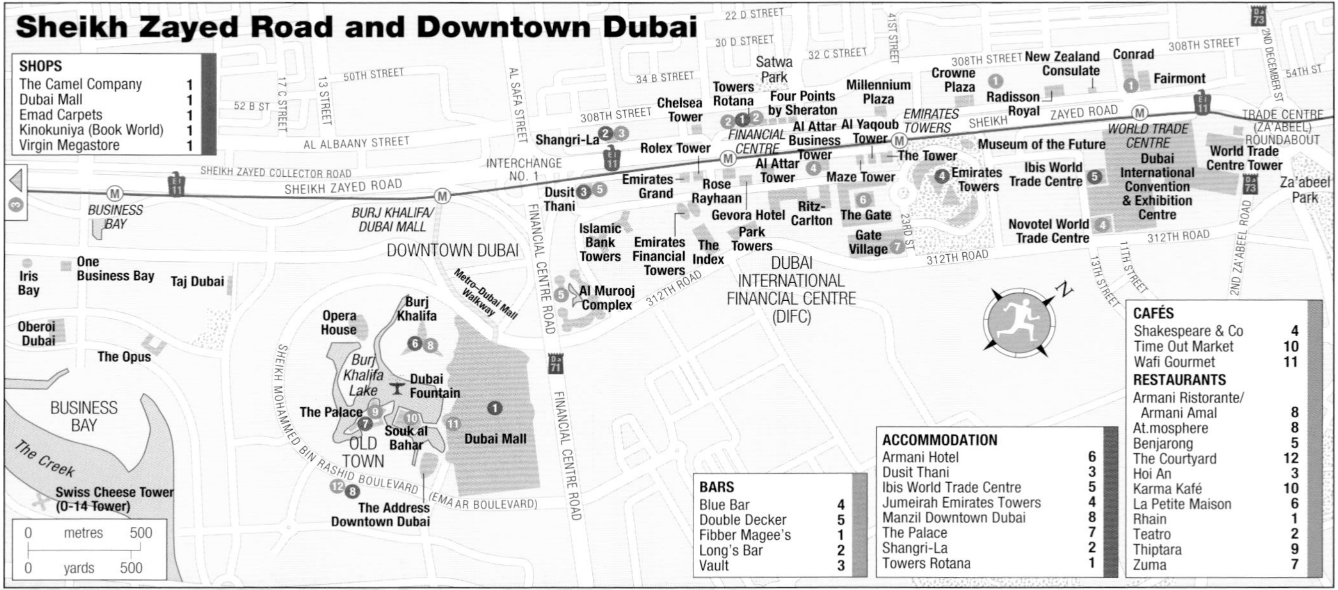
Sheikh Zayed Road and Downtown Dubai
SHOPS
The Camel Company 1
Dubai Mall 1
Emad Carpets 1
Kinokuniya (Book World) 1
Virgin Megastore 1
BARS
Blue Bar 4
Double Decker 5
Fibber Magee's 1
Long's Bar 2
Vault 3
ACCOMMODATION
Armani Hotel 6
Dusit Thani 3
Ibis World Trade Centre 5
Jumeirah Emirates Towers 4
Manzil Downtown Dubai 8
The Palace 7
Shangri-La 2
Towers Rotana 1
CAFÉS
Shakespeare & Co 4
Time Out Market 10
Wafi Gourmet 11
RESTAURANTS
Armani Ristorante/ Armani Amal 8
At.mosphere 8
Benjarong 5
The Courtyard 12
Hoi An 3
Karma Kafé 10
La Petite Maison 6
Rhain 1
Teatro 2
Thiptara 9
Zuma 7
SHEIKH ZAYED ROAD
SHEIKH ZAYED COLLECTOR ROAD
FINANCIAL CENTRE ROAD
DOWNTOWN DUBAI
DUBAI INTERNATIONAL FINANCIAL CENTRE (DIFC)
BUSINESS BAY
The Creek
OLD TOWN
Burj Khalifa
Dubai Mall
Dubai Fountain
Burj Khalifa Lake
Opera House
Souk al Bahar
The Palace
The Address Downtown Dubai
Metro–Dubai Mall Walkway
SHEIKH MOHAMMED BIN RASHID BOULEVARD
(EMAAR BOULEVARD)
Swiss Cheese Tower (0-14 Tower)
The Opus
Oberoi Dubai
Iris Bay
One Business Bay
Taj Dubai
BURJ KHALIFA/ DUBAI MALL
INTERCHANGE NO. 1
Al Murooj Complex
Islamic Bank Towers
Emirates Financial Towers
The Index
Park Towers
Gevora Hotel
Ritz-Carlton
The Gate
Gate Village
Emirates Grand
Dusit Thani
Shangri-La
Rolex Tower
Rose Rayhaan
Chelsea Tower
Towers Rotana
Four Points by Sheraton
Al Attar Business Tower
Al Attar Tower
Al Yaqoub Tower
Maze Tower
The Tower
Millennium Plaza
Crowne Plaza
Radisson Royal
New Zealand Consulate
Conrad
Fairmont
EMIRATES TOWERS
Emirates Towers
Museum of the Future
Ibis World Trade Centre
Novotel World Trade Centre
WORLD TRADE CENTRE
Dubai International Convention & Exhibition Centre
World Trade Centre Tower
TRADE CENTRE (ZA'ABEEL) ROUNDABOUT
Za'abeel Park
FINANCIAL CENTRE
Satwa Park
50TH STREET
13 STREET
17 C STREET
52 B ST
AL ALBAANY STREET
AL SAFA STREET
34 B STREET
308TH STREET
30 D STREET
22 D STREET
32 C STREET
41ST STREET
2ND DECEMBER ST
54TH ST
2ND ZA'ABEEL ROAD
312TH ROAD
23RD ST
13TH STREET
11TH STREET
N
0 metres 500
0 yards 500

Blvd), Downtown Dubai. Burj Khalifa/Dubai Mall metro ⓣ 04 888 8888, ⓦ burjkhalifa.ae. At the Top tours depart from the ticket desk in the lower-ground floor of the Dubai Mall (daily 8.30am–6pm). Prices vary according to the time of day, rising during the prime sunset hours (4–6pm) and costing from 160dh if prebooked online or From 399dh for At the Top Sky Experience tickets.

Rising imperiously skywards at the southern end of Sheikh Zayed Road stands the needle-thin **Burj Khalifa**, the world's tallest building. Opened in early 2010 after five years' intensive construction, the Burj finally topped out at a staggering 828m (2717ft), comprehensively smashing all existing world records. The astonishing scale of the Burj is difficult to fully comprehend – the building is best appreciated at a distance, from where you can properly appreciate its jaw-dropping height.

Access to the Burj Khalifa is strictly controlled. Most visitors opt for a visit to the "At the Top" observation deck on floor 124, offering sensational views; alternatively, the seriously pricey "At the Top Sky Experience" gives you access to a second, even loftier observation deck on floor 148, although the slight gain in height doesn't really justify the crazy ticket price. The tour also includes some interesting displays on the creation of the tower.

Dubai Mall

MAP P.52, POCKET MAP E5–F5
Financial Centre Rd. Burj Khalifa/Dubai Mall metro ⓦ thedubaimall.com.

Right next to the Burj Khalifa is the supersized **Dubai Mall**, with over 1200 shops spread across four floors and covering over a million square metres – making it easily the largest mall in the world measured by total area. Attractions here include the Dubai Aquarium (see below), and an Olympic-sized ice rink, while the mall's "Souk" area provides an incongruous home for the "Dubai Dino", an almost perfectly intact skeleton of a 150-million-year-old *Diplodocus longus*. Look out too for the eye-catching **The Waterfall**, complete with life-sized statues of fibreglass divers.

Dubai Aquarium and Underwater Zoo

MAP P.52, POCKET MAP F5
Dubai Mall. Burj Khalifa/Dubai Mall metro, ⓦ thedubaiaquarium.com.

Assuming you enter the Dubai Mall's main entrance off Financial Centre Road, one of the first things you'll see is the spectacular viewing panel of the **Dubai Aquarium and Underwater Zoo**: a huge, transparent floor-to-ceiling aquarium filled to the brim with fish big and small, including some large and spectacularly ugly grouper.

Dubai Fountain

Dubai Fountain

MAP P.52, POCKET MAP E5
Burj Khalifa Lake, Downtown Dubai. Burj Khalifa/Dubai Mall metro, bit.ly/TheDubaiFountain.

Winding through the heart of Downtown Dubai is the large **Burj Khalifa Lake**, a section of which doubles as the spectacular 275m-long (902ft) **Dubai Fountain**, the world's biggest, capable of shooting jets of water up to 150m (492ft) high, and illuminated with over 6000 lights and 25 colour projectors. The fountain really comes to life after dark, spouting carefully choreographed watery flourishes which "dance" elegantly in time to a range of Arabic, Hindi and classical songs, viewable from anywhere around the lake for free. Short (25min) **abra** rides around the lake/fountain are also available (daily 5.45–11.30pm; 65dh), leaving from outside the main lake-facing entrance to the Dubai Mall.

Old Town

MAP P.52, POCKET MAP E5
Burj Khalifa/Dubai Mall metro. Souk Al Bahar.

The chintzy **Old Town** development comprises a low-rise sprawl of sand-coloured buildings with traditional Moorish styling. Centrepiece is the **Souk al Bahar**, a small, Arabian-themed mall, pleasantly peaceful after neighbouring Dubai Mall. A string of restaurants lines the waterfront terrace outside, offering peerless views of Burj Khalifa.

Business Bay

MAP P.52, POCKET MAP C4–D5
Business Bay metro.

Directly south of Downtown Dubai, the shiny **Business Bay** development comprises a further dense cluster of high-rises arranged around the Dubal Water Canal, which can also be explored from here either on foot or by bike or boat (see page 62). As the name suggests the area is aimed at corporate rather than tourist types, although there are a few local landmarks worth a quick look. Close to the metro, the **JW Marriott Marquis Dubai** (355m/1099ft) was the world's tallest hotel until the Gevora (see page 51) nabbed its record in 2018. Several other weirdly shaped buildings line the road, including the eye-catching, crescent-shaped **Iris Bay**.

East of here, **The Opus**, by renowned Iraqi architect Zaha Hadid, is a huge, sinuously sculpted mass of dark glass, while further south lies the funky O-14 building, popularly known as the **Swiss Cheese Tower** thanks to the undulating layer of white cladding that envelops the entire structure, dotted with around 1300 circular holes and looking uncannily like an enormous piece of postmodern Emmenthal cheese.

Souk al Bahar

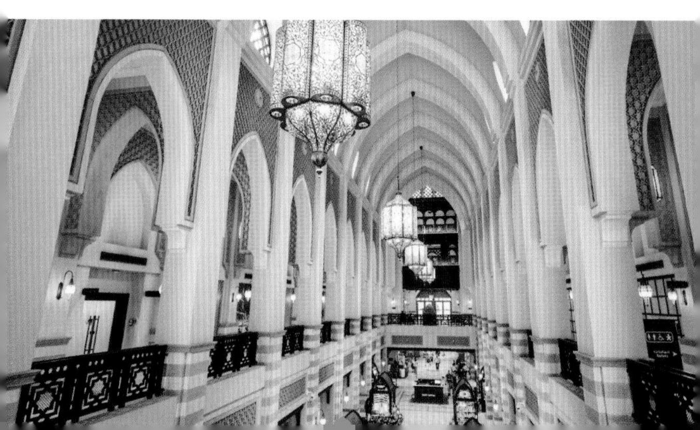

Shops

The Camel Company

MAP P.52, POCKET MAP E5
Downtown Dubai. Burj Khalifa/Dubai Mall metro Ⓦ thedubaimall.com.
Dubai's cutest selection of stuffed toy camels, plus assorted dromedary-themed stationery, mugs, cards, T-shirts and so on.

Dubai Mall

MAP P.52, POCKET MAP E5–F5
Downtown Dubai. Burj Khalifa/Dubai Mall metro Ⓦ thedubaimall.com.
Highlights in this mother of all malls include the flagship Bloomingdale's and Galeries Lafayette department stores; "Fashion Avenue", home to the biggest array of designer labels in Dubai; and the attractively chintzy "Souk" area, with a further 120 shops selling gold, jewellery and Arabian perfumes. Upstairs you'll find a Dubai branch of Hamleys, the famous London toyshop, alongside; Kinokuniya and Virgin (see below).

Emad Carpets

MAP P.52, POCKET MAP E5
The Souk, Dubai Mall. Burj Khalifa/Dubai Mall metro. Ⓣ 050 367 5606.
One of the city's leading carpet retailers, with gorgeous rugs (with prices to match) from Iran, Turkey, Afghanistan, Central Asia and Pakistan, plus kilims and pashminas.

Kinokuniya (Book World)

MAP P.52, POCKET MAP E5
Second floor, Dubai Mall. Burj Khalifa/Dubai Mall metro Ⓣ 04 434 0111.
This local outpost of the famous Japanese chain is far and away Dubai's best bookshop – a vast emporium stuffed with a simply massive array of titles, ranging from mainstream novels, travel guides and magazines through to graphic novels and a brilliant manga selection.

Dubai Mall

Virgin Megastore

MAP P.52, POCKET MAP E5
Dubai Mall. Burj Khalifa/Dubai Mall metro, Ⓦ virginmegastore.me.
This Dubai offshoot of the defunct UK chain sells all sort of electronics and gadgets but is mainly of interest for its excellent CD selection, with music from across the Middle east, plus recordings by many Gulf and Emirati artists.

Cafés

Shakespeare & Co

MAP P.52, POCKET MAP G4
South side of Al Saqr Business Tower, 37th St, off Sheikh Zayed Rd, roughly opposite the Ritz-Carlton Hotel. Financial Centre metro, Ⓦ shakespeare-and-co.com.
The original branch of a citywide café-cum-coffee-shop chain, characterized by its distinctively chintzy decor – a kind of high-camp Victoriana, with cherubs. Food includes a wide selection of breakfasts, soups, salads, sandwiches and crêpes, plus more substantial mains. There are two further branches nearby in the

Dubai Mall and Souk al Bahar, plus other locations citywide. DhDh

Time Out Market

MAP P.52, POCKET MAP E5
Souk al Bahar. Burj Khalifa/Dubai Mall metro. timeoutmarket.com/dubai.
On the top floor of Souk al Bahar, this innovative food court brings together a regularly changing array of local culinary talent from leading restaurants handpicked by the editors of the city's *Time Out* magazine, with 17 different outlets and three bars, plus a breezy outdoor terrace, offering the chance to sample some of Dubai's best foodie offerings under a single roof, and at prices significantly below what you'll pay in the city's top restaurants. DhDh

Wafi Gourmet

MAP P.52, POCKET MAP E5
Dubai Mall. Burj Khalifa/Dubai Mall metro, wafigourmet.com.
A brilliant waterside location in front of the Dubai Fountain is the main draw at this branch of the local deli-plus-café chain (see page 47), although you'll have to arrive early or get lucky to bag one of the coveted fountain-facing tables. Food features mouthwatering local delicacies, a great range of authentic mezze and more substantial Lebanese-style seafood and meat grills. DhDh

Restaurants

Armani Ristorante/ Armani Amal

MAP P.52, POCKET MAP E4
Burj Khalifa. Burj Khalifa/Dubai Mall metro, dubai.armanihotels.com.
There are a number of very upmarket dining options tucked away inside the suave *Armani* hotel. Top billing goes to the signature *Armani Ristorante*, overlooking the Dubai Fountain and serving fine-dining regional Italian cuisine (mains 145–325dh), while *Armani Amal* (closed Sun) also gets good

A table at Benjarong

reviews for its inventive regional Indian cuisine with a European twist. Note that if you're not staying at the hotel you'll need an advance reservation to gain admittance. DhDhDhDh

At.mosphere

MAP P.52, POCKET MAP H3
Burj Khalifa, Downtown Dubai. Burj Khalifa/Dubai Mall metro, ⓦ atmosphereburjkhalifa.com.
At.mosphere's selling point couldn't be simpler: this is the world's highest bar and restaurant, located almost half a kilometre above ground level on the 122nd floor of the soaring Burj Khalifa. Decor is svelte and modern, although your eyes will inevitably be drawn to the huge views outside. Prices are predictably sky-high. Come for breakfast, dinner or a spectacular afternoon tea (the latter is served daily from 12.30–4.30pm) in the more laidback attached lounge. Expect to pay more if dining at a window table. DhDhDhDh

Benjarong

MAP P.52, POCKET MAP F4
Dusit Thani Hotel, Sheikh Zayed Rd. Financial Centre metro ⓣ 04 317 4515.
Set in a delicately painted wooden pavilion on the 24th floor of the *Dusit Thani*, *Benjarong* offers some of the best Royal Thai cooking in Dubai. There's a particularly good selection of fish and seafood, plus the usual meat stir-fries and red and yellow curries, and they also do a lively Friday brunch. DhDhDh

The Courtyard

MAP P.52, POCKET MAP E5
Manzil Downtown Hotel, Sheikh Mohammed Bin Rashed Blvd. Burj Khalifa/Dubai Mall metro, ⓦ vidahotels.com.
Serene courtyard restaurant in the Arabian-theme Mazil Downtown hotel. The ambience is lovely and the menu features a savoury array of hot and cold mezze (with good vegetarian choices) plus assorted Arabian, Indian and international meat (plus a few fish) mains. DhDhDh

Hoi An

MAP P.52, POCKET MAP E5
Shangri-La hotel, Sheikh Zayed Rd. Financial Centre metro, ⓦ shangri-la.com.
Hybrid Vietnamese–French cuisine is the speciality here, served in an elegant colonial-style restaurant. Traditional Vietnamese dishes are combined with modern cooking techniques to produce unusual creations like the signature sea bass in lotus leaf with galangal and kumquat compote. DhDhDh

Karma Kafé

MAP P.52, POCKET MAP E5
Souk al Bahar. Burj Khalifa/Dubai Mall metro, ⓦ karma-kafe.com.
Sister establishment to the ever-popular *Buddha Bar* (see page 78), with a vaguely Japanese-looking interior and pleasant outdoor terrace. Food is mainly Japanese, alongside a few Chinese and Korean offerings, with plenty of *sashimi*, *nigiri*, *robata*, wagyu and stir-fries. There's a good drinks and cocktail list, too. DhDhDh

La Petite Maison

MAP P.52, POCKET MAP G4
Building 8, Gate Village, DIFC. Emirates Towers metro, ⓦ lpmlondon.co.uk/dubai.
An offshoot of the famous Nice restaurant, this is as authentic as European restaurants come in the UAE, offering traditional French cuisine in a bright white dining room which feels pleasantly traditional without being excessively starchy. Dishes include Gallic classics like snails and *canard à l'orange* alongside more Mediterranean-style offerings like gnocchi and beef ragout pasta. Reservations are usually essential. DhDhDh

Rhain

MAP P.52, POCKET MAP H3
Conrad Hotel, Sheikh Zayed Rd. World Trade Centre metro, ⓦ rhaindubai.com.

Thiptara

Rub shoulders with Dubai's glitterati at this extravagant restaurant which does its best to turn the simple business of cooking and eating into a full-blown theatrical experience, complete with open kitchen, tableside food prep and "show butcher". The menu ticks off pretty much every cliché of conspicuous consumption – foie gras, beluga caviar, lobster – and with mains from around 200dh you'll probably have to be a supermodel to afford it. For the full OTT experience book in for a Thursday, when there's also a live DJ and assorted live performers. DhDhDhDh

Teatro

MAP P.52, POCKET MAP G3

Towers Rotana Hotel, Sheikh Zayed Rd. Financial Centre metro, rotana.com.

This long-running Sheikh Zayed Rd favourite is one of the strip's livelier and more affordable offerings, with theatrically themed decor and a mix-and-match menu (mains 80–185dh) featuring a range of Southeast Asian, Chinese, Italian and Indian – anything from pizzas to butter chicken to lobster linguini – plus sushi and sashimi, all competently prepared and reasonably priced. DhDh

Thiptara

MAP P.52, POCKET MAP E5

The Palace Hotel, Old Town. Burj Khalifa/Dubai Mall metro, theaddress.com/en/restaurant/thiptara.

This beautiful Thai restaurant offers probably the best night-time view of the Burj Khalifa and Dubai Fountain. The menu is strongest on seafood, but also offers a fair spread of meat dishes (though few veg options). Reservations recommended. DhDhDhDh

Zuma

MAP P.52, POCKET MAP G4

Gate Village, Building 6. Emirates Towers metro, zumarestaurant.com.

Very hip Japanese bar-restaurant with a dining area (including sushi counter and *robata* grill) downstairs, and a bar-lounge above. Informal *izakaya*-style dining is the order of the day, with dishes designed to be shared, allowing you to mix and match items as you fancy from the top-notch selection of sushi, *sashimi, maki, nigiri.* DJs nightly from around 9pm. Reservations are usually essential. DhDhDhDh

Bars

Blue Bar

MAP P.52, POCKET MAP H4
Novotel, World Trade Centre. World Trade Centre metro, ⓦ facebook.com/BlueBarDubai.
This stylish little bar is a pleasant spot for a mellow drink earlier in the evening, with a sedate crowd and a good selection of speciality Belgian beers, plus cocktails, wines, premium whiskies and superior bar meals. The bar also hosts a wide range of live music acts, mainly jazz and blues – check their Facebook page for upcoming events.

Double Decker

MAP P.52, POCKET MAP F4
Al Murooj Rotana Hotel, Financial Centre Rd. Financial Centre metro, ⓦ facebook.com/DoubleDeckerMeOfficial.
One of the liveliest pubs in town, with quirky decor themed after the old London Routemaster buses and usually busy with a tanked-up crowd of expats and Western tourists. Live music and/or DJ most nights from around 9pm.

Fibber Magee's

MAP P.52, POCKET MAP H3
Off Sheikh Zayed Rd. Emirates Towers metro, ⓦ fibbersdubai.com.
One of the city's best-kept secrets, and probably Dubai's most impressive stab at a traditional European pub, with a spacious, very nicely done out wood-beamed interior and a good selection of draught beers including Kilkenny, Guinness, London Pride and Peroni, plus Magners cider. There's also regular live music and good, homely pub food. To reach it, go down the small side road between *Jashan* restaurant and *Zoom* (just south of the *Radisson* hotel) and it's on your left in the bottom of the *Stables* restaurant building.

Long's Bar

MAP P.52, POCKET MAP G3
Towers Rotana Hotel, Sheikh Zayed Rd. Financial Centre metro, ⓦ rotanatimes.com/towersrotana/dining/104.
Proud home to the longest bar in the Middle East, this English-style pub offers one of the strip's more convivial and downmarket drinking holes, with all the usual tipples and the ubiquitous TV sports.

Vault

MAP P.52, POCKET MAP C4
72nd floor, JW Marriott Marquis Hotel, Business Bay. Business Bay metro, ⓦ jwmarriottmarquisdubailife.com.
Dubai's second-highest bar, perched at the summit of the world's second-tallest hotel and offering 360º views through floor-to-ceiling windows. Fancy cocktails, bespoke spirits and fat cigars come as standard, although the daily 5–7pm happy hour keeps things a little more real. Regular DJs or live music Tues–Sat from 10pm.

Blue Bar

Jumeirah

A couple of kilometres south of the Creek, the beachside suburb of Jumeirah marks the beginning of southern Dubai's endless suburban sprawl, with swathes of chintzy low-rise villas providing a home to many of the city's European expats and other upper-income residents. The suburb is strung out along the Jumeirah Road, which arrows straight down the coast and provides the area with its principal focus, lined with a long string of shopping malls including the quirky, Italian-themed Mercato. Cultural attractions include guided tours of the impressive Jumeirah Mosque and visits to the Majlis Ghorfat um al Sheif, the former summer retreat of Dubai's erstwhile ruler Sheikh Rashid, while more hedonistic diversions can be found at Jumeirah Beach Park and the fun new La Mer development.

Jumeirah Mosque

MAP P.61, POCKET MAP H1
Jumeirah Rd. Bus #8, #88, #C10 and #X28.
Ⓦ jumeirahmosque.ae.

Rising proudly above the northern end of the Jumeirah Road, the stately **Jumeirah Mosque** is one of the largest and most attractive in the city, built in quasi-Fatimid (Egyptian) style, with a pair of soaring minarets, a roofline embellished with delicately carved miniature domes and richly decorated windows set in elaborate rectangular recesses. As with many of Dubai's more venerable-looking buildings though, medieval appearances are deceptive – the mosque was actually built in 1979.

No longer the case Regular **tours of the mosque** run by the Sheikh Mohammed Centre for Cultural Understanding (see page 27) offer a great opportunity to get a look at the mosque's rather florid interior, with its distinctive green-and-orange colour scheme and delicately painted arches, although the real draw is the informative guides, who explain some of the basic precepts and practices of Islam before inviting questions. The attached **Once Upon A Time** museum (free), showcases a beautiful selection of vintage Dubaian artefacts, lovingly presented. Modest dress is required so ensure to cover your shoulders and legs; head scarves are also provided free for ladies, or bring your own. Under-5s are not allowed; no pre-booking required for tours.

La Mer

MAP P.61, POCKET MAP G1
45 2 A Street Bus #8, #88, #C10 and #X28.
Ⓦ lamerdubai.ae/en. Free.

Just south of Jumeriah Mosque, the stylish **La Mer** beachside development offers a one-stop day-by-the-waves destination, with a fine swathe of sand equipped with changing huts and showers and a big selection of places to eat and drink, plus the obligatory slew of shops – although parts of the complex are currently being redeveloped as the **J1 Beach** complex, due to open in late 2023.

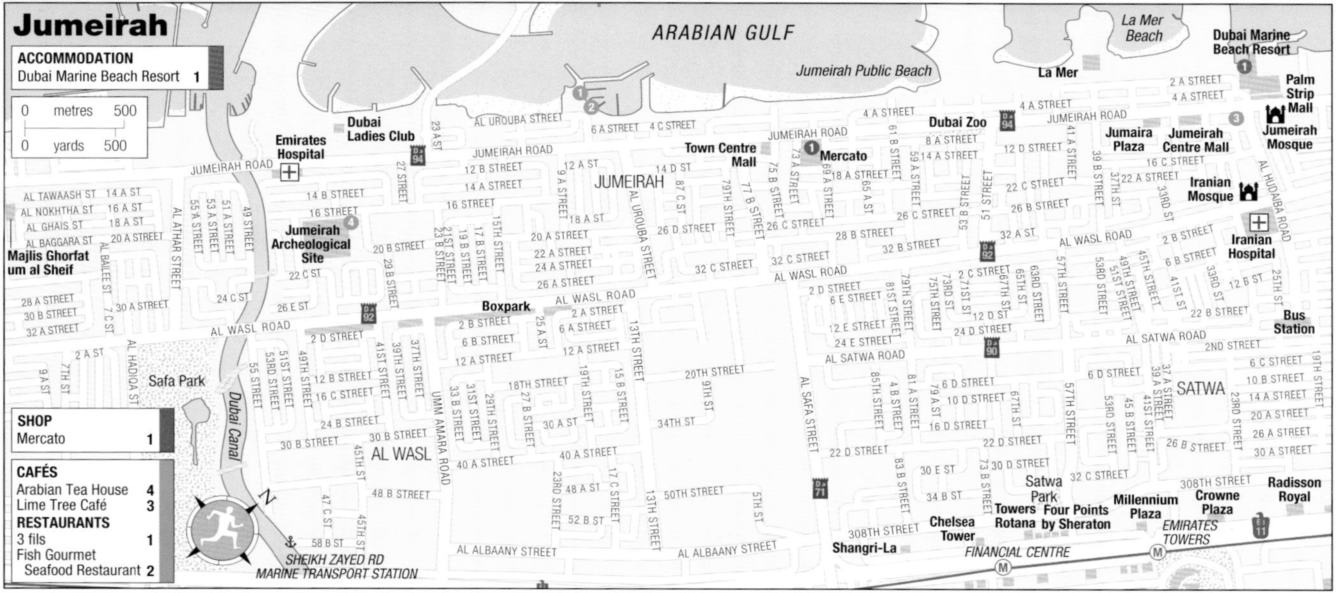
Jumeirah
ACCOMMODATION
Dubai Marine Beach Resort 1
0 metres 500
0 yards 500
SHOP
Mercato 1
CAFÉS
Arabian Tea House 4
Lime Tree Café 3
RESTAURANTS
3 fils 1
Fish Gourmet Seafood Restaurant 2
ARABIAN GULF
Jumeirah Public Beach
La Mer Beach
La Mer
Dubai Marine Beach Resort
Palm Strip Mall
Jumeirah Mosque
Jumaira Plaza
Jumeirah Centre Mall
Iranian Mosque
Iranian Hospital
Bus Station
Dubai Zoo
Mercato
Town Centre Mall
JUMEIRAH
Dubai Ladies Club
Emirates Hospital
Jumeirah Archeological Site
Majlis Ghorfat um al Sheif
Boxpark
Safa Park
Dubai Canal
AL WASL
SATWA
Satwa Park
Towers Rotana
Four Points by Sheraton
Millennium Plaza
Crowne Plaza
Radisson Royal
Chelsea Tower
Shangri-La
EMIRATES TOWERS
FINANCIAL CENTRE
SHEIKH ZAYED RD MARINE TRANSPORT STATION
JUMEIRAH ROAD
AL WASL ROAD
AL SATWA ROAD
AL SAFA STREET
AL UROUBA STREET
UMM AMARA ROAD
AL ALBAANY STREET
AL HUDAIBA ROAD
AL ATHAR STREET
AL HADIQA ST
N

Mercato

MAP P.61, POCKET MAP E1
Jumeirah Rd. Bus #8, #88, #C10 and #X28. Ⓦ mercatoshoppingmall.com.

About halfway down Jumeirah Road, the eye-popping **Mercato** mall looks like a kind of miniature medieval Italian city rebuilt by the Disney Corporation. Brightly coloured quasi-Venetian-cum-Tuscan palazzi are arranged around a huge central atrium overlooked by panoramic balconies – a memorable example of the sort of brazen kitsch that Dubai does so well.

Majlis Ghorfat um al Sheif

MAP P.61, POCKET MAP A1
17 St Bus #8, #88, #C10 and #X28. Ⓣ 04 852 1374.

Tucked away off the southern end of Jumeirah Road, the **Majlis Ghorfat um al Sheif** offers a touching memento of old Dubai, now incongruously marooned amid a sea of modern villas. Built in 1955 when Jumeirah was no more than a small fishing village, this modest traditional house – a simple two-storey coral-and-gypsum building embellished with fine doors and window shutters made of solid teak – was formerly used by Sheikh Rashid, the inspiration behind modern Dubai's spectacular development, as a summer house.

Dubai Water Canal

MAP P.61, POCKET MAP C1
Jumeirah Rd. Bus #8, #88 and #X28. Bike hire: Ⓦ bikeshopdubai.com's outlet at Business Bay is conveniently located for bike rentals. Abra cruises along the canal are available from Sheikh Zayed Rd Marine Transport Station (45min–1hr).

Opened in 2017, the **Dubai Water Canal** heads inland from the southern end of Jumeirah, running pass Safa Park and then snaking between the skyscrapers of Business Bay (see page 54) before reaching Ras al Khor (see page 46) where it connects with the southern end of the Creek, forming an unbroken waterway encircling a significant portion of the central city. A 6.4km walkway and cycle path runs along both sides of the canal, offering an enjoyably traffic-free place to stretch your legs or spin your wheels, with impressive skyscraper views on route plus a sequence of striking pedestrianized bridges including the ingenious Twisted Bridge and the graceful Bridge of Tolerance. You can charter the entire boat or pay per person with a minimum of eight passengers needed.

Majlis Ghorfat um al Sheif

Shop

Mercato

MAP P.61, POCKET MAP E1
Jumeirah Rd. Bus #8, #88 and #X28.
mercatoshoppingmall.com.
This kitsch Italian-themed mall packs in a good selection of rather upmarket outlets aimed at affluent local villa dwellers, including a decent range of mainstream designer labels.

Cafés

Arabian Tea House

MAP P.61, POCKET MAP C2
Jumeirah Archaeological Site, 16th St. Bus #8 or #C10.
arabianteahouse.com.
An offshoot of the Arabian Tea House in Bastakiya (see page 32), and with the same menu, this is an unexpected find in the sleepy backstreets of Jumeirah, offering a welcome retreat amidst the endless swathes of upmarket villas. The adjacent Jumeirah Archeological Site preserves the low-key remains of an old Abbasid settlement, with traces of ruined walls and stumps of columns dating back to the ninth century. DhDh

Lime Tree Café

MAP P.61, POCKET MAP H1
Jumeirah Rd. 04 325 6325,
thelimetreecafe.com.
Eternally popular with Jumeirah's expat wives and ladies-who-lunch, this cheery little establishment is a great place to people-watch, while the healthy menu includes moreish wraps, focaccias, panini, quiches and salads. It does a great selection of cakes, served in generous slices (also available to go). Make sure to order one of the freshly made juices. To date, it has six further outlets dotted across the city, although none of them are a patch on the original. DhDh

Mercato

Restaurants

3 fils

MAP P.61, POCKET MAP D1
Jumeirah Fish Market. Bus #8 or #C10.
3fils.com.
Winner of the inaugural Best Restaurant in MENA award in 2022, 3 fils has been wowing diners with its revolutionary (for Dubai) combination of Michelin-standard cuisine served in a humble, café-like setting at giveaway prices. The menu focuses on Japanese seafood alongside a selection of more international-style meat offerings, all artfully prepared with inventive use of the finest ingredients, including seafood flown directly from Tokyo's Tsukiji Market. Mix and match from the various small plates. Note that reservations are only accepted for the "chef's table", so you'll likely have to queue. DhDh

Fish Gourmet Seafood Restaurant

MAP P.61, POCKET MAP D1
Jumeirah Fish Market. Bus #8 or #C10.
fishgourmet.ae.
One of a number of unpretentious restaurants clustered around Jumeirah's two low-key fishing harbours, serving up excellent and eminently affordable seafood fresh from the waves, with plenty of grilled shrimp, calamari, salmon, sea bream and more. DhDh

The Burj al Arab and around

Some 18km (11 miles) south of the Creek, the suburb of Umm Suqeim marks the beginning of Dubai's spectacular modern beachside developments, announced with a flourish by three of Dubai's most famous landmarks: the iconic sail-shaped *Burj al Arab* hotel, the roller-coaster-like *Jumeirah Beach Hotel* and the fantastical Madinat Jumeirah complex. There are further attractions at the thrills-and-spills Wild Wadi water park and at Ski Dubai, the Middle East's first ski slope, while more sedentary pleasures can be found at the vast Mall of the Emirates, next to Ski Dubai, offering superbly surreal views of whose the snowy pistes. Close to the Mall of the Emirates on the far side of Sheikh Zayed Road, the industrial area of Al Quoz provides an unlikely home to a number of Dubai's leading art galleries.

The Burj al Arab

MAP P.66, POCKET MAP K15

Off Jumeirah Rd, Umm Suqeim. Bus #8, #88 and #X28. ⓦ burj-al-arab.com.

Rising majestically from its own man-made island just off the coast of Umm Suqeim is the peerless **Burj al Arab** ("Tower of the Arabs"). Commissioned by Dubai's ruler, Sheikh Mohammed, the aim of the Burj was simple: to serve as a global icon which would put Dubai on the international map. Money was no object. The total cost of the hotel was perhaps as much as $2 billion, and it's been

The splendid interior of the Burj al Arab

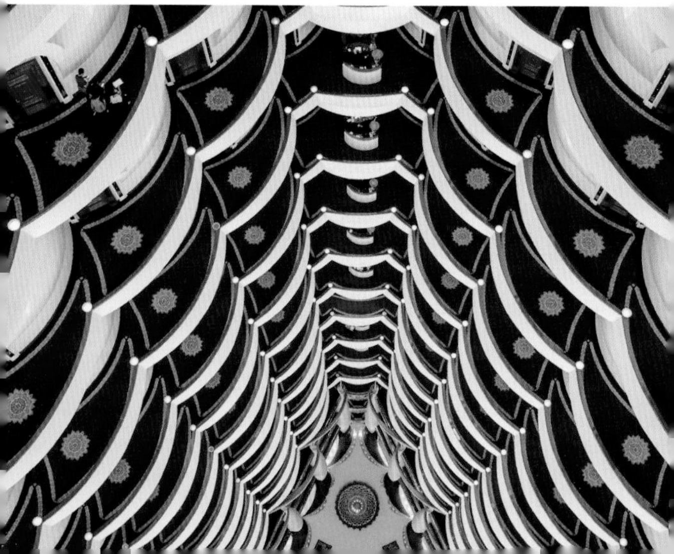

Visiting the Burj al Arab

Non-guests are only allowed into the *Burj* on one of the hotel's various packages (advance booking essential). The cheapest option is to sign up for a guided tour (various options available; details at Ⓦ insideburjalarab.com; from 249dh). Alternatively, make a **reservation** (phone Ⓣ 800 32 32 32, email Ⓔ restaurants@jumeirah.com) at one of the hotel's bars or restaurants. Big spenders might enjoy the hotel's two fine-dining restaurants: the **Ristorante L'Olivo at Al Mahara** (see page 70) or **Al Muntaha**, at the very top of the building, while there are several other slightly less wallet-draining restaurants available – or have a drink or a sumptuous afternoon tea at either the **Sahn Eddar** lobby lounge (minimum spend 290dh; afternoon teas 400/560dh) or the **Skyview Bar** (minimum spend 200dh), perched at the summit of the hotel. Other options include a visit to the gorgeous Talise spa (treatments from 600dh) or spend a day on the private beach terrace (Mon–Thurs 800dh, Fri–Sun 1000dh – with half the cost redeemable on foods and drinks).

estimated that even if every room in it remains full for the next hundred years, the Burj still won't pay back its original investment.

Sheikh Mo's bold gamble paid off handsomely, and the building's instantly recognizable outline quickly established itself as a global symbol of Dubai to rival the Eiffel Tower, Big Ben and the Sydney Opera House. Even the top-floor helipad has acquired celebrity status: André Agassi and Roger Federer once famously played tennis on it, while Tiger Woods used it as a makeshift driving range, punting shots into the sea.

The Burj is home to the world's first so-called **seven-star hotel**, an expression coined by a visiting journalist to emphasize the unique levels of luxury offered within. Designed to echo the shape of a dhow's sail, the hotel's shore-facing side mainly comprises a huge sheet of white Teflon-coated fibreglass cloth, which is spectacularly illuminated by night. Most of the **interior** is actually hollow, consisting of an enormous atrium vibrantly coloured in great swathes of red, blue and green, supported by massive, bulbous golden columns.

Staying at the *Burj al Arab* is a very expensive pleasure, and even just visiting presents certain challenges. Fortunately, the building's magnificent exterior can be enjoyed for free from numerous vantage points nearby.

Jumeirah Beach Hotel

MAP P.66, POCKET MAP L15

Jumeirah Rd, Umm Suqeim. Bus #8, #88 and #X28. Ⓦ jumeirah.com.

The huge **Jumeirah Beach Hotel** (or "JBH") is the second of the area's landmark buildings, after the Burj al Arab. Designed to resemble an enormous breaking wave (although it looks more like an enormous roller coaster) and rising to a height of over 100m (328ft), the hotel was considered the most spectacular and luxurious in the city when it opened in 1997, although it has since been overtaken on both counts. It remains a fine sight, however, especially when seen from a distance in combination with the Burj al Arab, right next door, against whose slender sail it appears (with a little imagination) to be about to crash.

Wild Wadi

MAP P.66, POCKET MAP L15
Off Jumeirah Rd, Umm Suqeim. Bus #8, #88 and #X28. Ⓦ wildwadi.com.

The massively popular **Wild Wadi** water park offers a variety of attractions to suit everyone from small kids to physically fit adrenaline junkies, complete with fantasy tropical lagoon, cascading waterfalls, whitewater rapids and hanging bridges. Get oriented with a circuit of the Whitewater Wadi (MasterBlaster) ride, which runs around the edge of the park, during which you're squirted on powerful jets of water up and down eleven long, twisting slides before being catapulted down the darkened Tunnel of Doom. Dedicated thrill-seekers should try the Wipeout and Riptide Flowriders, simulating powerful surfing waves, and the park's stellar attraction, the **Jumeirah Sceirah**, one of the world's highest waterslides.

Madinat Jumeirah

MAP P.66, POCKET MAP K15–16
Al Sufouh Rd, Al Sufouh. Bus #8, #88 and #X28. Ⓦ madinatjumeirah.com.

A vast mass of faux-Moorish-style buildings, the huge **Madinat Jumeirah** complex rises high above the coastal highway. Opened in 2005, the Madinat is one of Dubai's most spectacular modern developments: a self-contained miniature "Arabian" city comprising a vast sprawl of sand-coloured buildings topped by an extraordinary quantity of wind towers, the whole thing arranged around a sequence of meandering palm-fringed waterways along which visitors are chauffeured in replica abras.

There's an undeniable whiff of Disneyland about the entire complex, admittedly, although the sheer scale of the place is strangely compelling. The Madinat also offers some of the most eye-boggling views in Dubai, with

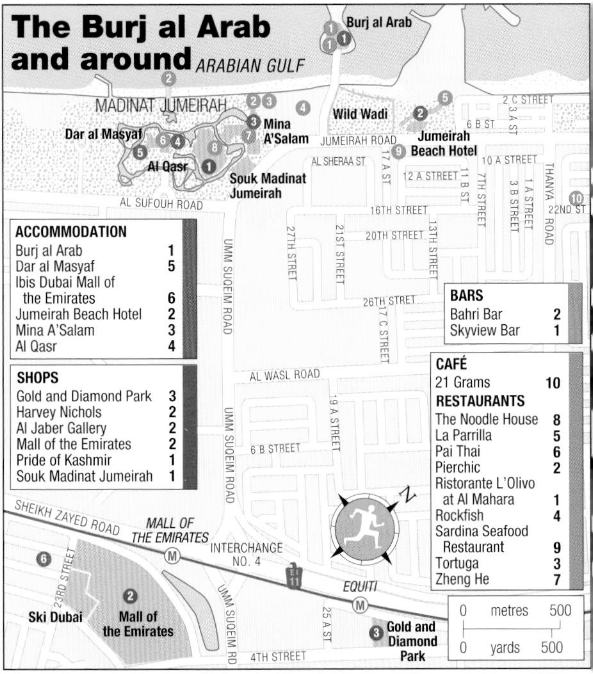

Madinat Jumeirah's stalls and abras

the futuristic outlines of the Burj al Arab surreally framed between medieval-looking wind towers and Moorish arcading.

The obvious place from which to explore the complex is the **Souk Madinat Jumeirah** (see page 68), though it's well worth investigating some of the superb restaurants and bars in the *Al Qasr* and *Mina A'Salam* hotels, several of which offer superlative views over the Madinat itself, the Burj al Arab and coastline.

Mall of the Emirates

MAP P.66, POCKET MAP J18–K18
Interchange 4, Sheikh Zayed Rd. Mall of the Emirates metro ⓦ malloftheemirates.com.
The second-largest mall in Dubai (outdone only by the Dubai Mall), the swanky **Mall of the Emirates** is one of the most popular in the city, packed with hundreds of shops and crowds of locals and tourists alike. For dedicated shopaholics it's one of the best places in Dubai to splash some cash (see page 68) – and there's also the added bonus of surreal views of the snow-covered slopes of Ski Dubai through huge glass walls at the western end of the mall, or from one of the various restaurants and bars overlooking the slopes).

Ski Dubai

MAP P.66, POCKET MAP J18
Mall of the Emirates, Interchange 4, Sheikh Zayed Rd. Mall of the Emirates metro, ⓦ skidxb.com.
Attached to the Mall of the Emirates, the huge **Ski Dubai** is unquestionably one of the city's weirder ideas: a huge indoor snow-covered ski slope complete with regular snowfall amid the sultry heat of the Gulf. Accredited skiers and snowboarders can use five runs of varying height, steepness and difficulty, including the world's first indoor black run. There's also a Ski academy for beginners and improvers, or just visit the Snow Park (220dh) to mess around in the white stuff – fun for smaller kids. Ski Dubai also has a troupe of resident King and Gentoo penguins. A couple can be seen for free from the mall during the regular "March of the Penguins" (every 2hr on the hour), or at closer quarters on a full-blown "Penguin Encounter" (see page 117). Avail of a two-hour lesson (pre-booking is usually essential) or buy a ski pass.

Shops

Gold and Diamond Park

MAP P.66, POCKET MAP L18
Sheikh Zayed Rd between interchanges 3 and 4. FGB metro, goldanddiamondpark.com.

This low-key little mall is the place to come if you want diamonds, which retail here for up to half the price you'd expect to pay back home. You'll also find a few other precious stones and platinum jewellery for sale, plus a small amount of gold. Some places can also knock up custom-made designs.

Harvey Nichols

MAP P.66, POCKET MAP J18
Mall of the Emirates. Mall of the Emirates metro, harveynichols.com.

The flagship shop of one of Dubai's flagship malls, this suave, minimalist three-storey department store offers a vast array of international labels, including British classics like Vivienne Westwood and Alexander McQueen.

Al Jaber Gallery

MAP P.66, POCKET MAP K2
Souk Madinat Jumeirah, aljabergallery.ae.

Dubai's leading purveyor of low-grade Arabian "handicrafts". Look hard enough and you might find some half-decent stuff, including attractive old traditional wooden boxes and coffee pots, though the shop is perhaps best regarded as a source of hilarious kitsch – think cheesy fridge magnets and garish "Aladdin lamps". Other branches at the Dubai Mall, Souk al Bahar and Marina Mall.

Mall of the Emirates

MAP P.66, POCKET MAP J18–K18
Interchange 4, Sheikh Zayed Rd. Mall of the Emirates metro malloftheemirates.com.

Among the best one-stop shopping destinations in the city (see page 67), with around five hundred stores to browse, good places to eat and drink, and the surreal snow-covered slopes of Ski Dubai to ogle.

Pride of Kashmir

MAP P.66, POCKET MAP J18
Souk Madinat Jumeirah. prideofkashmir.com.

One of the city's leading handicrafts chains, more upmarket than Al Jaber Gallery (see above) but perfectly affordable. Stock usually includes carpets and kilims alongside assorted antiques, pashminas and traditional-style wooden furniture. There's a second branch at Souk al Bahar.

Souk Madinat Jumeirah

MAP P.66, POCKET MAP K16
Madinat Jumeirah.

At the heart of the Madinat Jumeirah, this superb re-creation of a "traditional" souk serves up a beguiling mix of shopping, eating and drinking opportunities, with a good selection of upmarket handicraft and souvenir outlets including Pride of Kashmir (see above). Like all good bazaars, the layout is mazy and disorienting, although you'll never be far from where you want to be.

Café

21 Grams

MAP P.66, POCKET MAP M2
Meyan Mall, Al Thanyah St, 21grams.me.

A complete change from the fancy hotel eateries nearby, this self-styled "Urban Balkan Bistro" showcases southeastern Europe's diverse cuisine, with dishes ranging from phyllo pie and moussaka to cabbage rolls and lamb shank slow cooked in milk. The attached bakery is great for take-outs. DhDh

The ultimate kitsch children's gift from the Camel Company

Restaurants

The Noodle House

MAP P.66, POCKET MAP K2

Madinat Jumeirah. ☎ 800 32 32 32.

A long-running Dubai favourite, this cheapish and very cheerful noodle bar serves a great selection of Chinese and Southeast Asian food including more-ish "street bites" and tasty main features classic dishes wok and rice dishes including nasi goreng, pad thai, Hookien mee and Hoisin chicken. DhDh

La Parrilla

MAP P.66, POCKET MAP L15

25th floor, Jumeirah Beach Hotel, Jumeirah Rd. ☎ 04 432 3232.

Perched atop the *Jumeirah Beach Hotel*, this Argentinian-themed steakhouse boasts superb views of the Burj al Arab, excellent Argentinian, Australian and Wagyu steaks (from around 200dh) and an appealing splash of Latin atmosphere, with live music and tango dancers nightly. DhDhDh

Pai Thai

MAP P.66, POCKET MAP K15

Dar al Masyaf Hotel, Madinat Jumeirah. ☎ 800 32 32 32.

This beautiful Thai restaurant is one of the city's most romantic places to eat, with stunning Burj al Arab views from the candlelit terrace and live music murmuring gently in the background. Food includes all the usual Thai classics, such as spicy salads, meat and seafood curries – not the most original menu in town, although given the setting you probably won't care. DhDhDhDh

Pierchic

MAP P.66, POCKET MAP K15

Al Qasr Hotel, Madinat Jumeirah.

The romantic waterside setting at Pierchic

ⓣ 800 32 32 32.

One of the city's most spectacularly situated restaurants, perched at the end of a breezy pier jutting out in front of the grandiose *Al Qasr* hotel, and with unbeatable views of the nearby Burj al Arab, *Jumeirah Beach Hotel* and Madinat Jumeirah (try to get a table on the terrace). The fine-dining Italian menu and scratchy service get mixed reviews – but the view, at least, can't be beaten. DhDhDhDh

Ristorante L'Olivo at Al Mahara

MAP P.66, POCKET MAP K1

Ground Floor, Burj al Arab. ⓣ 800 32 32 32.

In the basement of the Burj, this is one of Dubai's oldest uber-deluxe restaurants: an intimate, low-lit space with tables arranged around a stunning circular aquarium – a bit like eating under the sea. Overseen by Michelin-starred chef Andrea Migliaccio, the superb European-style seafood is amongst the best in the city – as it should be. DhDhDhDh

Rockfish

MAP P.66, POCKET MAP K1

Jumeirah Al Naseem Hotel. ⓣ 800 32 32 32.

Soothing beachfront restaurant at the upmarket new Jumeirah Al Naseem hotel dishing up some of Dubai's finest Mediterranean-style cuisine. Seafood takes centre stage on the menu, but there are also good meat and pasta options – anything from lobster risotto to chicken cacciatora. And there's also a relatively affordable three-course lunch menu. DhDhDhDh

Sardina Seafood Restaurant

MAP P.66, POCKET MAP L2

The Mall, Jumeirah Rd. ⓦ sardina.ae.

Unpretentious establishment opposite Jumeirah Beach Hotel serving super-fresh local seafood at bargain prices, either grilled or baked or featuring Middle Eastern preparations including seafood tajines and Egyptian-style *singary* (butterflied fish filled with a zesty tomato-based sauce). Prices are by weight so you can choose exactly how much you want to eat. Dh

Tortuga

MAP P.66, POCKET MAP K15

Mina A'Salam Hotel, Madinat Jumeirah. ⓣ 800 32 32 32.

Lively Mexican restaurant complete with obligatory Mariachi band Food features the usual Mexican standards (mains from 105dh) including quesadillas, fajitas and burritos – or check out the live taco station, with fillings customized to your choice. DhDhDh

Zheng He

MAP P.66, POCKET MAP K15

Mina A'Salam Hotel, Madinat Jumeirah. ⓣ 800 32 32 32.

Classy Chinese restaurant dishing up top-notch fine dining (mainly Cantonese, with a splash of Szechuan). There's nothing particularly innovative about the menu, although quality is high and the setting memorable, with seating either inside the svelte restaurant or outside on the beautiful Burj-facing terrace. DhDhDh

Bars

Bahri Bar

MAP P.66, POCKET MAP K15

Mina A'Salam, Madinat Jumeirah. ⓣ 800 32 32 32.

Superb little Arabian-style outdoor terrace, liberally scattered with canopied sofas, Moorish artefacts and Persian carpets, and offering drop-dead gorgeous views of the Burj and Madinat Jumeirah – particularly beautiful towards sunset.

Skyview Bar

MAP P.66, POCKET MAP K15

27th Floor, Burj al Arab.

ⓔ restaurants@jumeirah.com.

Landmark bar perched near the summit of the Burj al Arab, with vast sea and city views – coming for a drink here is currently the cheapest way to see the inside of this fabulous hotel. The huge drinks list majors in cocktails, but also sports a decent spread of wines, spirits, mocktails and even a few beers. Minimum spend 200dh per person; advance reservations essential.

Bahri Bar

The Palm Jumeirah and Dubai Marina

Nowhere is the scale of Dubai's explosive growth as staggeringly obvious as in the far south of the city, home to the vast Palm Jumeirah artificial island and Dubai Marina development – evidence of the emirate's magical ability to turn sand into skyscrapers and raise entire new city suburbs up out of the waves. In the early 2000s this whole area was more or less desert. Then the developers moved in. By mid-decade the district had turned into the largest construction site on the planet. Ten years on and the cranes and building crews have gone, leaving a brand-new city and the world's largest man-made island in their wake, with a forest of densely packed skyscrapers lined up around the glitzy marina itself.

The Palm Jumeirah

MAP P.74, POCKET MAP D10–G15
Monorail trains every 15min.

Lying off the coast around 5km south of the Burj al Arab and stretching 4km (2.5 miles) out into the waters of the Arabian Gulf, **The Palm Jumeirah** – the biggest artificial island in the world – has doubled the length of the Dubai coastline at a total cost of over $12 billion. As its name suggests, the Palm Jumeirah is designed in the shape of a palm tree, with a central "trunk" and a series of sixteen radiating "fronds", the whole enclosed in an 11km-long (7 miles)

Palm Jumeirah

Dubai's artificial islands

For a city with aspirations of taking over the world's tourism industry, Dubai has a serious lack of one thing: **coastline**. In its natural state, the emirate boasts a mere 70km of shoreline, totally insufficient for its various needs. Dubai's solution to its pressing lack of waterfront was characteristically bold: it decided to build some more. The Palm Jumeirah was just the first (and smallest) of the proposed offshore developments. Two further palm-shaped islands – the **Palm Jebel Ali**, 20km further down the coast, and the gargantuan **Palm Deira**, right next to the old city centre – were also planned through billion-dollar land reclamation projects. The latter never materialized, despite a second failed attempt to relaunch as "Deira Islands. It was finally taken over by the Nakheel Group and is now quipped to become **Dubai Islands**, a work currently in progress and due to finalize in 2026. Visitors can expect on completion a 20km extension of the city's coastline, dotted, of course, with Blue-flag beaches, golf courses with views across the Arabian Gulf, a mega mall, parkland and marinas. The world's largest market – Souk Al Marfa is set to be here too, alongside resident housing, a hotel resort with multiple restaurants and a waterpark. Watch this space...

breakwater, or "crescent", lined with a string of huge, upmarket resorts.

The best way to see the Palm is from the **Palm Jumeirah Monorail**, whose driverless trains shuttle along an elevated track between the *Atlantis* resort and the mainland, offering sweeping views over the Palm. The mainland terminus of the monorail connects to Palm Jumeirah station on the Dubai Tram network.

Atlantis

POCKET MAP E10–F10

Crescent Rd, Palm Jumeirah, Ⓦ atlantis.com/dubai. Monorail trains every 15min.

At the furthest end of the Palm Jumeirah, the vast **Atlantis** resort is the island's major landmark: an outlandish pink colossus perched over the sea like some kind of weird triumphal arch. What it lacks in architectural taste, it does at least partly make up for in on-site facilities and (pricey) activities. Best is the spectacular **Aquaventure** water park, featuring an adrenaline-charged array of rides and slides centred on the dramatic "Ziggurat", where you'll find the park's headline Leap of Faith waterslide, 27.5m (90.2ft) tall, which catapults you at stomach-churning speed down into a transparent tunnel amid a lagoon full of sharks.

The Lost Chambers aquarium

Alternatively, head to **The Lost Chambers**, a sequence of halls and tunnels running through the hotel's vast underground aquarium, populated by an extraordinary array of 65,000-odd tropical fish and dotted with assorted "ruins".

Dubai Marina

MAP P.74, POCKET MAP A15–D16
Sobha Realty or DMCC metros.

A vast phalanx of tightly packed high-rises signals the appearance of **Dubai Marina**, Dubai's brand-new city-within-a-city, built at lightning speed since 2005. Like much of modern Dubai, the marina is a mishmash of the good, the bad and the downright ugly. Many of the high-rises are of minimal architectural distinction, and all are packed so closely together that the overall effect is of hyperactive urban development gone completely mad. The whole area feels oddly piecemeal and under-planned, while the lack of pedestrian facilities (excepting the pleasant oceanfront The Walk at JBR and Marina Walk; see page 75) means that you're unlikely to see much more of it than can be glimpsed while speeding down Sheikh Zayed Road by car or metro.

It's weirdly impressive, even so, especially by night, when darkness hides the worst examples of gimcrack design and the whole area lights up into a fabulous display of airy neon.

Jumeirah Beach Residence and The Walk

MAP P.74, POCKET MAP A15–B15
Sobha Realty metro. Covent Garden.

Most of Dubai Marina's tourist development is focused on the string of luxurious **beachside hotels** which established themselves here when the coast was largely undeveloped, but now

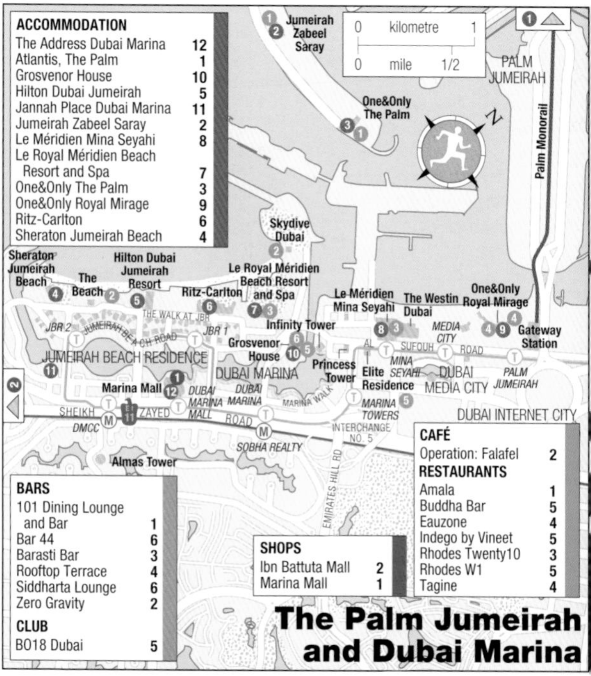

Free beaches

If you want to laze by the sea but aren't staying in a resort with its own private beach, the go-to destination is **Dubai Marina Beach**, an expansive swathe of **free sand** between the *Sheraton* and *Hilton* hotels. The beach is also good for watersports, available through either Sky & Sea (@ watersportsdubai.com) or Water Adventure Dubai (@ wateradventure.ae), both with kiosks on the beach behind the *Sheraton* hotel and offering activities including windsurfing, sailing, kayaking, waterskiing, wake-boarding, parasailing and jet-skiing.

find themselves tragically hemmed in by densely packed high-rises on all sides. Notable among these is the unlovely **Jumeirah Beach Residence** (**JBR**): a 1.7km-long sprawl of forty high-rises with living space for ten thousand people. The JBR's one redeeming feature is **The Walk at JBR**, an attractive promenade lined with boutiques, cafes and restaurants, while slightly further along the attractive (and attractively low-rise) **The Beach** complex (@ thebeach.ae) offers a further slew of restaurant and retails options. The market opens from October to April.

Marina Walk

MAP P.74, POCKET MAP B16–C16
Sobha Realty or DMCC metros.

Dubai's **marina** is actually a man-made sea inlet, lined with luxury yachts and fancy speedboats, which snakes inland behind the JBR, running parallel with the coast for around 1.5km (0.9 miles). Encircling the water is the attractive pedestrianized promenade known as **Marina Walk**, its long straggle of waterfront cafés and restaurants enjoyably lively after dark. Presiding over the northern sea inlet into the marina is the quirky **Infinity Tower** (330m/1083ft),

Marina Beach

Dubai: the world's tallest city

Dubai is now officially the tallest city on the planet, currently home to thirteen of the world's 100 highest buildings (it's nearest rival, Shenzen, has eleven), more than double the number found in traditional high-rise hotspots such as New York, Chicago, Hong Kong and Shanghai. The landmark example of Dubai's sky-high ambition is provided by the staggering Burj Khalifa (see page 51), while other high-rise icons include the Burj al Arab (see page 64) and the glittering Emirates Towers (see page 50), as well as less-well-known buildings such as the slender *Gevora* (see page 51), the world's tallest hotel.

instantly recognizable thanks to its distinctively twisted outline which rotates through 90 degrees from base to summit – a bit like the famous Turning Tower in Malmö, Sweden.

Various kiosks around Marina Walk offer a mix of expensive **boat** charters alongside much cheaper dhow cruises for those who want to take to the water.

Ain Dubai

POCKET MAP A15
Bluewaters Island, Dubai Marina. DMCC metro, or bus F57 from Jebel Ali metro. ⓦ aindubai.com/en.

Facing the Marina on Bluewaters Island, **Ain Dubai** is the world's tallest ferris wheel – almost a carbon-copy of the older London Eye – albeit almost twice as tall (250m/820ft). A ride on the wheel lasts around forty minutes, offering unparalleled views over new Dubai, from the massed skyscrapers of the Marina to the arcing fronds of the Palm Jumeirah artificial island and beyond – astonishing enough in itself, even

Marina Walk

Starbucks, Ibn Battuta Mall

more so when you consider that less than twenty years ago there was virtually nothing here bar empty desert and untamed sea.

Ibn Battuta Mall

POCKET MAP A16
Ibn Battuta metro
ⓦ ibnbattutamall.com.
The outlandish, mile-long **Ibn Battuta Mall** is undoubtedly Dubai's wackiest shopping experience. The mall is themed in six different sections after some of the places – Morocco, Andalucia, Tunisia, Persia, India and China – visited by the famous Arab traveller Ibn Battuta. Highlights include a life-sized elephant complete with mechanical mahout (rider), a twilit Tunisian village and a full-sized Chinese junk, while the lavishness of some of the decoration would seem more appropriate on a Rajput palace or a Persian grand mosque than a motorway mall.

Expo City Dubai

Expo 2020 metro.
ⓦ expocitydubai.com, free.
The ground-breaking Dubai Expo 2020 (although it was actually held in 2021–22 due to Covid) was one of most spectacular in the history of the global exhibition series and the first ever held in the Middle East, transforming over four square kilometres (1.5 square miles) of former desert at the southern edge of Dubai into a futuristic hub at a cost of around $8bn. Many of the Expo's largest structures have been left in place and are now being repurposed as Expo City Dubai, a major new commerical, conference and tourist hub. Highlights include the flagship Al Wasl Plaza, a vast metallic dome lit up with spectacular laser displays after dark (although shows are currently paused), the dramatic Alif Mobility Pavilion by Foster + Partners, the aptly named Surreal (a kind of fountain which flows upwards), and the Garden in the Sky observation tower (30dh), aka as "The Flying Park".

Shops

Ibn Battuta Mall

MAP P.74, POCKET MAP A16
Between interchanges 5 and 6, Sheikh Zayed Rd. Ibn Battuta metro
ibnbattutamall.com.

This Ibn Battuta-inspired mall is worth a visit for its stunning decor alone (see page 77) – although as a shopping experience it's a bit underpowered. Shops include a handy Borders bookstore and a well-stocked branch of the local Toy For Less chain– and check out the entertaining Daiso in the Andalucia court, a kind of Japanese pound shop.

Marina Mall

MAP P.74, POCKET MAP B16
Sheikh Zayed Rd. Jumeirah Lakes Towers metro marinamall.ae.

Dubai's newest and swankiest mall, with a big selection of mainly upmarket outlets – the big central atrium looks like a kind of postmodern temple of designer brands. There's also a good selection of cafés in the water-facing side and in the attached Pier 7 tower.

Eauzone

Café

Operation: Falafel

MAP P.74, POCKET MAP A15
The Beach Mall, Dubai Marina. Jumeirah Beach Residence 2 tram
operationfalafel.com.

Arm yourself with a fork, don your food-vision goggles and get ready for Operation: Falafel, a bright modern café chain whose creators have tasked themselves with the mission of bringing good, inexpensive traditional Arabian street food to cities across the world. Offerings include a great selection of regional favourites, freshly prepared using quality ingredients – crunchy sambousek pastries, creamy moutabal, halloumi wraps, flavoursome zaatar and of course lots of falafel. Dh

Restaurants

Amala

MAP P.74, POCKET MAP C13
Jumeirah Zabeel Saray Hotel, Palm Jumeirah. 04 453 0444.

The most popular of the *Zabeel Saray*'s stunning collection of restaurants, as opulently decorated as a Bollywood film set and with good, quite reasonably priced food (mains 65–140dh), and a mainly North Indian menu featuring classics like butter chicken and mutton *rogan josh* alongside a good vegetarian selection. DhDhDh

Buddha Bar

MAP P.74, POCKET MAP C16
Grosvenor House Hotel, Dubai Marina. DAMAC Properties metro 04 317 6000, buddhabar-dubai.com.

Modelled after the famous Parisian joint, this superb bar-restaurant is a sight in its own right: a huge, sepulchral space hung with dozens of red-lantern chandeliers. The menu features

Indego by Vineet

a fine array of Japanese and pan-Asian cooking – pricey, but worth it for the ambience. Advance reservations recommended. DhDhDhDh

Eauzone

MAP P.74, POCKET MAP E15
Arabian Courtyard, One&Only Royal Mirage Hotel, Dubai Marina. Palm Jumeirah tram station, royalmirage.oneandonlyresorts.com.
Regularly voted Dubai's most romantic restaurant, with seating amid the beautifully floodlit waters of one of the hotel's swimming pools and a short but sweet menu (mains 135–200dh) of Japanese-style meat and seafood mains (but no vegetarian options). Reserve ahead. DhDhDhDh

Indego by Vineet

MAP P.74, POCKET MAP C15
Grosvenor House Hotel, Dubai Marina. Sobha Realty metro, indegobyvineet.com.
Overseen by Vineet Bhatia, India's first Michelin-starred chef, this stylish restaurant showcases his contemporary Indian cooking, blending subcontinental and international ingredients and techniques to unusual effect. DhDhDhDh

Rhodes Twenty10

MAP P.74, POCKET MAP C15
Le Royal Méridien Hotel, Dubai Marina. DAMAC Properties metro, leroyalmeridien-dubai.com.
Casual and affordable, Gary Rhodes' second Dubai restaurant features succulent grills, steaks and seafood alongside British classics like fish 'n' chips with mushy peas and Manchester Scotch eggs. DhDhDh

Rhodes W1

MAP P.74, POCKET MAP C15
Grosvenor House Hotel, Dubai Marina. DAMAC Properties metro, rw1-dubai.com.
Gary Rhodes' original Dubai restaurant décor focuses on quality covers of European classics served in a casual atmosphere – fisherman's pie, chicken kiev, mushroom risotto and so on, and they also do a fine Sunday "Rhoast" (geddit?). DhDhDh

Tagine

MAP P.74, POCKET MAP E15
The Palace, One&Only Royal Mirage Hotel, Dubai Marina. Media City tram station, royalmirage.oneandonlyresorts.com.
Sumptuous little Moroccan restaurant, the beautiful Moorish decor complemented by authentic North African cooking including classics like pigeon *pastilla* pie, Marrakech-style *tangia* and a selection of delicious tagines. DhDhDh

Bars

101 Dining Lounge and Bar

MAP P.74, POCKET MAP C14
One&Only The Palm Hotel, Palm Jumeirah. thepalm.oneandonlyresorts.com.
Overlooking the swish new *One&Only The Palm*'s private marina, *101*'s big draws are its gorgeous terrace over the water outside (live DJ most evenings) and stunning views across to the marina's skyscrapers opposite.

Bar 44

MAP P.74, POCKET MAP C15
44th floor, Grosvenor House Hotel, Dubai Marina. Sobha Realty metro, bar44-dubai.com.
This svelte contemporary bar offers peerless 360-degree views of the entire marina development, with twinkling high-rises stretching away in every direction and a big selection of wallet-emptying champagnes and cool cocktails.

Barasti Bar

MAP P.74, POCKET MAP D15
Le Méridien Mina Sehayi Hotel, Dubai Marina. Mina Seyahi tram station barastibeach.com.
A Dubai institution, celebrating its 30th birthday in 2025, this fun, two-level beachside bar continues to pull in one of the city's most eclectic crowds and is likely to be a favourite. Downstairs is usually more Ibiza chill-out, with ambient music, shisha and loungers on the sand; the pubbier upstairs is generally noisier, with live DJs and a party atmosphere.

The bar in Rhodes W1

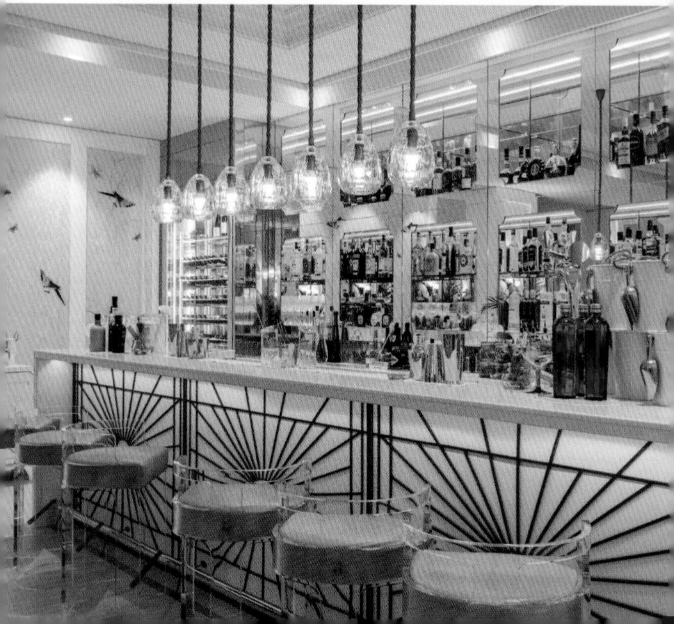

Rooftop Terrace

Rooftop Terrace

MAP P.74, POCKET MAP E15
Arabian Court, One&Only Royal Mirage Hotel, Dubai Marina. Media City tram station, royalmirage.oneandonlyresorts.com.
One of Dubai's ultimate Orientalist fantasies, with seductive Moorish decor, cushion-strewn pavilions, silver-tray tables and other assorted Arabiah artefacts. A smooth live DJ adds to the *One Thousand and One Nights* ambience.

Siddharta Lounge

MAP P.74, POCKET MAP C16
Tower Two, Grosvenor House Hotel. Dubai Marina metro, siddhartalounge.com.
Cool poolside terrace and bar – a great place to relax and catch some breezes at the end of a long hot day. There's also a good selection of Asian and Mediterranean-style light meals and snacks. Shisha available from 5pm.

Zero Gravity

MAP P.74, POCKET MAP C15
Sky Dive Dubai Drop Zone, Al Sufouh Rd. Sobha Realty metro. 0-gravity.ae.
This chilled-out venue doesn't quite know whether it's a bar, restaurant, beach-club or live-music venue, but does all of them pretty well. Choose between a beach lounger (with sweeping marina views), the garden behind (with stage hosting regular live music acts) or the funky dining room and circular bar inside. There's a good drinks list at sensible prices, plus a wide-ranging international menu.

Club

B018 Dubai

MAP P.74, POCKET MAP D16
Level 42, Media One Hotel, Al Falak St. Al Khail metro. b018dxb.com.
Winner of Time Out's Best Club in Dubai award in 2022, this offshoot of the famous Lebanese venue is one of the city's go-to nightspots. Grab a drink in the lush "Tropical Room" (from 6pm) before heading to the "Main Room" later on (whose industrial aesthetic was inspired by a wartime Beirut bunker) where DJs churn out a variety of sounds ranging from soul and disco to classic house, garage and techno.

Sharjah

Just 10km (6 miles) north up the coast, the city of Sharjah seems at first sight like simply an extension of Dubai, with whose northern suburbs it now merges seamlessly in an ugly concrete sprawl. Physically, the two cities may have virtually fused into one, but culturally they remain light years apart. Sharjah has a distinctively different flavour, having clung much more firmly to its traditional Islamic roots, exemplified by a fine array of museums devoted to various aspects of Islamic culture and local Emirati life. These include the world-class Museum of Islamic Civilization, the excellent Sharjah Art Gallery, the impressive Sharjah Heritage Museum, and the engaging Al Mahatta aviation museum. Other attractions include the massive Blue Souk and Souq al Arsa.

Sharjah Museum of Islamic Civilization

MAP P.84

Corniche St, sharjahmuseums.ae.

The main reason for trekking out to Sharjah is to visit the superb **Sharjah Museum of Islamic Civilization**, which occupies the beautifully restored waterfront Souk al Majara building, topped with a distinctive golden dome. The museum is spread over two levels. Downstairs, the **Abu Bakr Gallery of Islamic Faith** has extensive displays on the elaborate rituals associated with the traditional Haj pilgrimage to Mecca, while the **Ibn al Haitham Gallery of Science and Technology** showcases the extensive contributions made by Arab scholars to scientific innovation over the centuries. The first floor of the museum is devoted to four galleries offering a chronological overview of **Islamic arts and crafts**, with superb displays of historic manuscripts, ceramics, glass, armour, woodwork, textiles and jewellery. Exhibits include the first-ever map of the then known world (i.e. Eurasia), created by Moroccan cartographer Al Shereef al Idrisi in 1099 – a surprisingly accurate document, although slightly baffling at first sight since it's oriented upside down, with south at the top.

Sharjah Creek

MAP P.84

Sharjah's broad **Creek** describes a leisurely parabola around the northern edge of the city centre before terminating in the expansive Khaled Lagoon. Despite being long since eclipsed by Dubai's various ports, Sharjah's Creek still sees a considerable amount of commercial shipping both modern and traditional, usually with a few old-fashioned wooden dhows moored up on the far side of the water beneath a long line of spiky gantries.

Sharjah Art Museum

MAP P.84

Clearly signed off Corniche St, or access from Al Burj Ave, behind Al Hisn fort, sharjahmuseums.ae, free.

Occupying a large modern wind-towered building, the **Sharjah Art Museum** is the major showpiece in Sharjah's attempts to position itself as a serious player in the international art scene.

Temporary exhibitions of varying quality feature on the ground floor. Upstairs, the museum's new permanent gallery of modern Arabian art holds a wide range of works created in the past four decades from countries across the region in an eclectic range of styles and media – all technically proficient, although none lingers long in the memory.

Al Hisn Fort

MAP P.84

Al Burj Ave, Ⓦ sharjahmuseums.ae.

At the heart of the city is the quaint **Al Hisn Fort** of 1820, the most enduring symbol of old Sharjah, formerly home to the ruling Al Qassimi family, although it's now ignominiously hemmed in by ugly apartment blocks. The extensively renovated building now looks neater, shinier and an awful lot cleaner than it ever did in the past, with a series of displays dotted around various rooms and a few atmospheric photographs of the fort in former years.

Heritage Area

MAP P.84

The area west of Al Hisn Fort was formerly the heart of old Sharjah, an old-fashioned quarter of traditional Emirati houses arranged around a sequence of spacious, lopsided squares and labyrinthine alleyways, and enclosed in a long section of reconstructed city wall. The entire area has now been meticulously renovated and relaunched as the city's so-called **Heritage Area**, home to several interesting museums and the Souq al Arsa.

Souq al Arsa and around

MAP P.84

Heritage Area.

Al Hisn Fort

The **Souq al Arsa**, which bounds the northern side of the Heritage Area, is far and away the prettiest in Sharjah, centred around an atmospheric central pillared courtyard, flanked by the personable little *Al Arsaha Public Coffee House* (see page 85). An intriguing tangle of alleyways radiates out from the courtyard, lined with coral-stone shops stuffed full of all sorts of colourful local handicrafts as well as an eclectic selection of curios and collectibles.

Tucked away around the back (north) side of the Souq al Arsa is the attractive **Majlis Ibrahim Mohammed al Madfa**, topped by a diminutive round wind tower, said to be the only one in the UAE.

Bait al Naboodah

MAP P.84

Opposite the Souq al Arsa, Heritage Area, ⓦ sharjahmuseums.ae.

The atmospheric old **Bait al Naboodah** offers an interesting re-creation of traditional family life in Sharjah. The main draw is the rambling two-storey building itself, one of the most attractive in the UAE, arranged around a spacious central courtyard with wooden doorways, leading into a series of bedrooms furnished in traditional Gulf style.

Sharjah Heritage Museum

MAP P.84

Heritage Area, ⓦ sharjahmuseums.ae.

The excellent **Sharjah Heritage Museum** is one of the best collections of its kind anywhere in the UAE. Wide-ranging and well-explained exhibits cover all the usual bases – traditional dress, architecture, social customs, the pearling trade and so on – with many insights into lesser-known local customs en route.

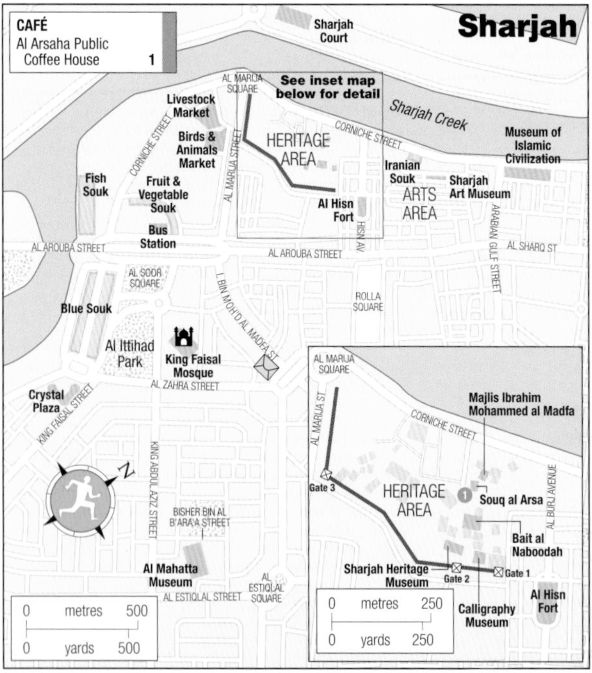

Blue Souk

The Blue Souk

MAP P.84

King Faisal St, 1km west of the city centre (about 12dh by taxi).

The huge **Blue Souk** (officially known as the Central Souk) occupies an enormous, eye-catching and ungainly pair of buildings topped by myriad wind towers and clad in brilliant blue tiling. The souk is best known for its numerous carpet shops, which stock a vast range of Persian and other rugs (usually) at significantly lower prices than in Dubai.

Al Mahatta Museum

MAP P.84

Bisher bin al Bara'a St (Street 23), off King Abdul Aziz St (around 15dh by taxi from the centre), ⓦ sharjahmuseums.ae.

Devoted to the history of aviation in Sharjah, the absorbing **Al Mahatta Museum** occupies the buildings of what was until 1977 the city's airport, complete with aircraft hangar and air traffic control tower (the runway was incorporated into what is now King Abdul Aziz Street). The cavernous **hangar** contains five antique planes dating from the 1930s to the 1950s, while the remainder of the museum occupies the old airport **rest house**, with fascinating displays about the first commercial flights to Sharjah (launched in 1932 by Imperial Airways) and other exhibits.

Café

Al Arsaha Public Coffee House

MAP P.84

Souq al Arsa.

This quaint little café offers a beguiling window on local life, with attractive decor in traditional Arabian style and an entertaining local clientele. It's a good place for a glass of mint tea or a cup of coffee, and they also serve up mountainous, spicy biriyanis (chicken, mutton or fish). Dh

Al Ain

For a complete change of pace, a day-trip out to the sedate desert city of Al Ain, some 130km (81 miles) inland (a two-hour minibus ride) from Dubai on the border with Oman, offers the perfect antidote to the rip-roaring pace of life on the coast. The UAE's fourth-largest city and only major inland settlement, Al Ain – and the twin city of Buraimi, on the Omani side of the border – grew up around the string of six oases whose densely packed swathes of palms still dot the modern city. The city served as an important staging post on trading routes between Oman and the Gulf, a fact attested to by the forts and rich archeological remains found in the vicinity.

Al Ain National Museum and around

MAP P.88

Off Zayed bin Sultan St. Closed for renovation at the time of writing.

The old-fashioned **Al Ain National Museum** is well worth a look before diving into the rest of the city. The first section sports the usual dusty displays on local life and culture, while the second offers a comprehensive overview of the archeology of the UAE.

Right next to the museum, the **Sultan bin Zayed Fort** (or Eastern Fort) is one of the eighteen or so scattered around Al Ain. The picturesque three-towered structure is best known as the childhood home of Sheikh Zayed bin Sultan al Nahyan (ruled 1966–2004), who oversaw the transformation of the emirate from impoverished Arabian backwater into today's oil-rich contemporary city-state.

Al Ain Oasis

MAP P.88

Between Al Ain St and Zayed bin Sultan St, south of the centre. Free.

A dusty green wall of palms announces the beautiful **Al Ain Oasis**, with a mazy network of little walled lanes running between the densely planted thickets of trees including an estimated 150,000-odd date palms. There are eight entrances dotted around the perimeter of the oasis, although given the disorienting tangle of roads within, you're unlikely to end up coming out where you entered.

Al Ain Souk

MAP P.88

Immediately in front of the bus station.

Al Ain Souk is home to the city's main meat, fruit and vegetable market. Housed in a long, functional warehouse-style building, the souk is stocked with the usual picturesque piles of produce, prettiest at the structure's west end, where Indian traders sit enthroned amid huge mounds of fruit and vegetables.

Al Ain Palace Museum

MAP P.88

Al Ain St, on the western side of Al Ain Oasis ☎ 03 711 8388. Free.

The **Al Ain Palace Museum** occupies one of the various forts around Al Ain owned by the ruling Nahyan family of Abu Dhabi. The sprawling complex is pleasant enough, with rambling, orangey-

A khanjar (dagger), Al Ain National Museum

pink buildings arranged around a sequence of five courtyards and small gardens, although the palace's thirty-odd rooms, including assorted bedrooms, *majlis* and a small school, aren't particularly interesting.

Jahili Fort

MAP P.88.
120th St, off Sultan bin Zayed al Awwal St. Free.

Of Al Ain's various mud-brick forts, **Jahili Fort**, built in 1898, is easily the most impressive, with a fine battlemented main tower and a spacious central courtyard. The much-photographed circular tower on the northern side – with four levels of diminishing size, each topped with a line of triangular battlements – probably predates the rest of the fort. Jahili Fort is also home to the excellent little **Mubarak bin London** exhibition, devoted to the life of legendary explorer **Wilfred Thesiger** (1910–2003). Thesiger – or Mubarak bin London (the "Blessed Son of London") as he was known to his Arab friends – stayed at the fort in the late 1940s at the end of one of the two pioneering journeys across the deserts of the Empty Quarter which later formed the centrepiece of *Arabian Sands*, his classic narrative of Middle Eastern exploration.

Hili Gardens and Archeological Park

About 8km north of the city. Free.

The **Hili Gardens and Archeological Park** is the site of one of the most important archeological sites in the UAE – many finds from here are displayed in the Al Ain Museum, which also provides a good explanation of their significance. The main surviving structure is the so-called "**Hili Grand Tomb**", a circular mausoleum dating from the third century BC, made from large, finely cut and fitted slabs of stones. A quaint carving of two people framed by a pair of long-horned oryx decorates the rear entrance.

Al Ain Zoo

Off Nahyan al Awwal St, around 7km southwest of the centre, alainzoo.ae.

The excellent **Al Ain Zoo** is a guaranteed crowd-pleaser for both kids and adults. There are over four thousand animals here, humanely housed in large open pens spread around the very spacious grounds. Inmates include plenty of African fauna – big cats, giraffes, zebras and rhinos (including rare South African white lions and Nubian giraffes) – along with numerous Arabian animals and birds. Free for children under 3 years.

Camel Souk

Off the Oman road, behind the Bawadi mall, about 10km from the city centre.

Al Ain's old-fashioned **Camel Souk** (actually just a series of pens in the open desert) is worth a visit, despite being a bit tricky to find, attracting a lively crowd of local camel-fanciers haggling over dozens of dromedaries lined up for sale, plus sheep and goats. The souk is busiest in the mornings before around 10am, although its often possible to see camels throughout the day. Be aware that there are some very pushy traders here who may demand massively inflated tips for showing you around or allowing you to take photographs of their animals. Always agree a sum in advance.

Jebel Hafeet

30km south of Al Ain on the Omani border.

The soaring 1180m **Jebel Hafeet** (or Hafit), the second-highest mountain in the UAE, is a popular retreat for locals wanting to escape the heat of the desert plains. You can drive in half an hour or less along an excellent road to the top, from where there are peerless views over the surrounding Hajar mountains. The outdoor terrace at the *Mercure Grand* hotel, perched just below the summit, makes a

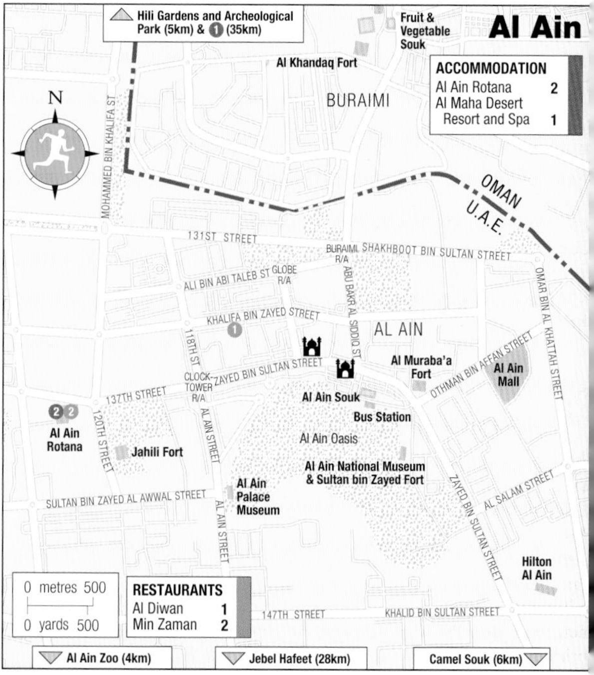

Oryxes in Dubai Desert Conservation Reserve

memorable – if often surprisingly chilly – spot for a drink. Taxis cost around 100dh.

Dubai Desert Conservation Reserve

E66 highway, around 50km from Dubai and 75km from Al Ain ⓦ ddcr.org.

For a taste of real, unadulterated UAE desert, it's well worth a visit to the superb **Dubai Desert Conservation Reserve**. The reserve encloses 250 square kilometres (108 square miles) of shifting dunes which serve as a refuge for over thirty local mammal and reptile species, including rare and endangered oryx and Arabian mountain gazelle. Tours can be arranged through various operators (see the reserve's website for full details) including Arabian Adventures, Travco and Alpha (see page 112) and there are also balloon flights over the reserve with Balloon Adventures Dubai (ballooning.ae). Alternatively, you can stay in the reserve at the idyllic but wickedly expensive *Al Maha* resort (see page 104).

Restaurants

Al Diwan

MAP P.88

Khalifa bin Zayed St ⓣ 03 764 4445.

Rustic-looking restaurant with very cheery staff and a menu of Lebanese, Iranian and European classics – grilled pigeon, kebabs, assorted mezze and a wide selection of (pricier) seafood. Most mains DhDh

Min Zaman

MAP P.88

Al Ain Rotana hotel, ⓦ rotana.com/alainrotana.

The swankiest Lebanese restaurant in town, offering a delicious range of authentic mezze, kebabs and salads, alongside other Middle Eastern staples. Sit either in the attractive dining room or on the terrace, with live singer most nights. DhDhDh

Abu Dhabi

The capital of the UAE, Abu Dhabi is the very model of a modern Gulf petro-city: thoroughly contemporary, shamelessly wealthy and decidedly staid. Abu Dhabi's lightning change from obscure fishing village into modern city-state within the past forty years is perhaps the most dramatic of the region's stories of oil-driven transformation, although for the casual visitor the city is mainly interesting for how it contrasts with its more famous neighbour – an Arabian Washington to Dubai's Las Vegas. Highlights include the stunning Sheikh Zayed Mosque, the new Louvre museum, and the flamboyant *Emirates Palace Hotel plus adjacent Qasr al Watan presidential palace*, while it's also worth exploring the modernist souk at the World Trade Center.

Emirates Palace Hotel

MAP P.92

Corniche Rd West, emiratespalace.com.

Standing in solitary splendour at the western end of the city is the vast **Emirates Palace Hotel**. Opened in 2005, it was intended to rival Dubai's *Burj al Arab* and provide Abu Dhabi with a similarly iconic "seven-star" landmark – although in fact the two buildings could hardly be more different. Driveways climb up through the grounds to the main entrance to the hotel, which sits in an elevated position above the sea and surrounding gardens. It's cleverly stage-managed, although the quasi-Arabian design is pretty generic and it's really only the sheer size of the complex (the main building measures around half a kilometre or 0.3 miles from end to end) which impresses. The **interior** is perhaps more memorable, centred on a dazzling central dome-cum-atrium, with vast quantities of marble and huge chandeliers. Non-guests can visit by booking in for the hotel's superb afternoon tea (see page 95) or a meal at one of its numerous restaurants –be sure to reserve in advance.

Emirates Palace Hotel

Qasr Al Watan

MAP P.92

Breakwater, qasralwatan.ae.

Immediately west of the Emirates Palace, the similarly flamboyant Qasr Al Watan (Presidential Palace) was completed in 2017 and opened to the public in 2019: a sprawling edifice constructed on the grandest scale and surrounded by vast plazas of gleaming polished marble. Inside, a sequence of dazzling ceremonial interiors project Emirati cultural and political prestige, including the vast domed Great Hall, the opulent Presidential Banquet and the soaring Al Barza meeting room – while visitors may also be allowed a glimpse into the "Spirit of Collaboration" conference space, home to meetings of the UAE cabinet and assorted leading regional organizations.

The Corniche

MAP P.92

Driving through Abu Dhabi's suburban sprawl, it's easy not to notice that the city is built on an island – at least until you emerge on the expansive **Corniche**, the sweeping waterfront road that runs for the best part of 5km (3 miles) along Abu Dhabi's western edge. The road is lined by spacious gardens on either side and flanked by a long line of glass-clad high-rises which both encapsulate the city's internationalist credentials and provide Abu Dhabi with its most memorable views.

Heritage Village

MAP P.92

Breakwater ⓣ 02 681 4455. Free.

Dramatically situated on the Breakwater – a small protuberance of reclaimed land jutting out from the southern end of the Corniche – the **Heritage Village** offers a slice of traditional Abu Dhabi done up for visiting coach parties.

The Corniche

The "village" consists of a line of picturesque *barasti* huts, including several **workshops** where local artisans – carpenters, potters, brass-makers and so on – can sometimes be seen at work, although the main attraction is the spectacular view over the water to the skyscrapers lining the Corniche.

Marina Mall

MAP P.92

Marina Village, Breakwater

ⓦ marinamall.ae.

Dominating the centre of the Breakwater, the large **Marina Mall** is a top shopping destination, and also offers fine views of the Corniche. These are best

Abu Dhabi transport

Regular express **buses** (4.30am–11.30pm; every 20–30min; 2hr–2hr 30min; 30dh) run from Al Ghubaiba bus station in Bur Dubai and Ibn Battuta metro station to Abu Dhabi's main bus station, about 3km (2 miles) inland from the city centre. A convenient alternative is to take a **tour** from Dubai. Numerous companies offer Abu Dhabi day-trips (see page 112), with prices starting from around 300dh. Abu Dhabi's various attractions are very spread out, but there are plenty of metered **taxis** around town (flag fare 5dh).

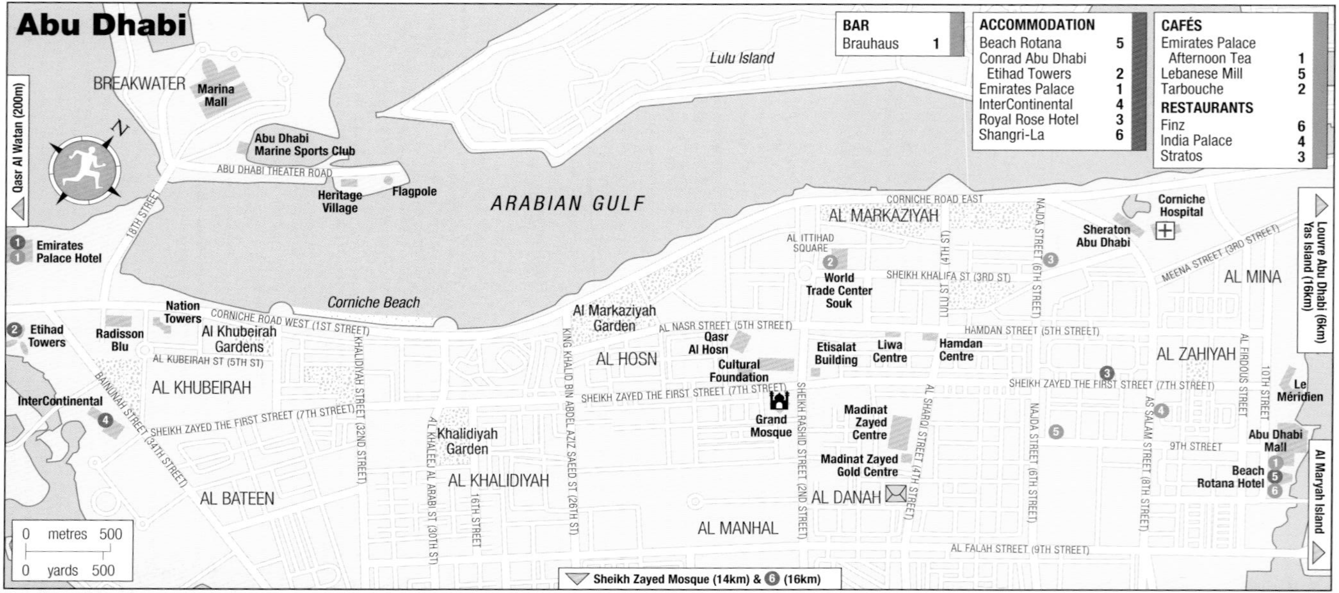
Abu Dhabi
BAR
Brauhaus 1
ACCOMMODATION
Beach Rotana 5
Conrad Abu Dhabi Etihad Towers 2
Emirates Palace 1
InterContinental 4
Royal Rose Hotel 3
Shangri-La 6
CAFÉS
Emirates Palace Afternoon Tea 1
Lebanese Mill 5
Tarbouche 2
RESTAURANTS
Finz 6
India Palace 4
Stratos 3
Lulu Island
BREAKWATER
Marina Mall
Abu Dhabi Marine Sports Club
ABU DHABI THEATER ROAD
Heritage Village
Flagpole
ARABIAN GULF
Qasr Al Watan (200m)
18TH STREET
Emirates Palace Hotel
Corniche Beach
Nation Towers
CORNICHE ROAD WEST (1ST STREET)
Etihad Towers
Radisson Blu
Al Khubeirah Gardens
AL KUBEIRAH ST (5TH ST)
AL KHUBEIRAH
InterContinental
BAINUNAH STREET (34TH STREET)
SHEIKH ZAYED THE FIRST STREET (7TH STREET)
AL BATEEN
KHALIDIYAH STREET (32ND STREET)
AL KHALEEJ AL ARABI ST (30TH ST)
Khalidiyah Garden
16TH STREET
AL KHALIDIYAH
KING KHALID BIN ABDEL AZIZ SAEED ST (26TH ST)
Al Markaziyah Garden
AL HOSN
AL NASR STREET (5TH STREET)
Qasr Al Hosn
Cultural Foundation
SHEIKH ZAYED THE FIRST STREET (7TH STREET)
Grand Mosque
SHEIKH RASHID STREET (2ND STREET)
AL MANHAL
AL MARKAZIYAH
CORNICHE ROAD EAST
AL ITTIHAD SQUARE
World Trade Center Souk
Etisalat Building
Liwa Centre
Hamdan Centre
Madinat Zayed Centre
Madinat Zayed Gold Centre
AL DANAH
AL SHARQI STREET (4TH STREET)
LULU ST (4TH ST)
SHEIKH KHALIFA ST (3RD ST)
HAMDAN STREET (5TH STREET)
NAJDA STREET (6TH STREET)
AL FALAH STREET (9TH STREET)
Sheraton Abu Dhabi
Corniche Hospital
MEENA STREET (3RD STREET)
AL MINA
AL ZAHIYAH
SHEIKH ZAYED THE FIRST STREET (7TH STREET)
AS SALAM STREET (8TH STREET)
AL FIRDOUS STREET
10TH STREET
9TH STREET
Le Méridien
Abu Dhabi Mall
Beach Rotana Hotel
Louvre Abu Dhabi (6km)
Yas Island (16km)
Al Maryah Island
Sheikh Zayed Mosque (14km) & 6 (16km)
0 metres 500
0 yards 500

appreciated from the soaring **Burj al Marina** tower at the back of the mall, which you can visit for the price of an expensive drink at the 41st-floor *Colombiano Coffee House*.

Qasr al Hosn and around

MAP P.92

Sheikh Rashid bin Saeed al Maktoum St ⓦ quasaralhosn.ae.

More or less at the very centre of Abu Dhabi sits **Qasr Al Hosn** ("The Palace Fort"), the oldest building in Abu Dhabi. The fort started life around 1761 as a single round watchtower built to defend the only freshwater well in Abu Dhabi, and was subsequently expanded, serving as the residence of Abu Dhabi's ruling Al Nahyan family right up until 1966. Reopened in 2018 after extensive renovation, the fort now hosts exhibits covering the history of the city, while local craftspeople can sometimes be seen at work in the House of Artisans – or head to the Bait al Gahwa ("House of Coffee") to enjoy a traditional Arabian coffee ceremony The sleek adjacent **Cultural Foundation** (ⓦ culturalfoundation.ae; same hours; free) hosts a range of exhibitions, workshops and performances.

World Trade Center and around

MAP P.92

Between Al Ittihad Square and Sheikh Khalifa St (3rd St) ⓦ wtcad.ae.

The huge **World Trade Center**, topped by a pair of shiny cylindrical skyscrapers, is one of the city's most interesting recent developments. The Center's main attraction is its marvellous **souk**, designed by Foster & Partners and offering a memorable postmodern take on the traditional Arabian bazaar.

On the southwestern side of the World Trade Center, **Al Ittihad Square** is home to an arresting sequence of oversized sculptures, including a vast cannon, enormous perfume bottle and gargantuan coffeepot – an endearingly quirky contrast to the humdrum surrounding architecture.

Al Maryah Island

MAP P.92

Immediately beyond downtown, on the far side of a narrow sea inlet, a cluster of dramatic skyscrapers

World Trade Center Souk

announce the city's new financial district, Al Maryah Island, Abu Dhabi's biggest and most futuristic urban development, centred on the dramatic Abu Dhabi Global Market Square, with four massive skyscrapers surrounding the distinctively anvil-shaped Abu Dhabi Global Market building, and the very chic waterside Galleria mall below.

Louvre Abu Dhabi

MAP P.92

Saadiyat Island, Bus 94; water taxi from Marsa Mina. ⓦ louvreabudhabi.ae.

Opened in 2017, Abu Dhabi's offshoot of the famous Paris museum is without doubt the city's most unusual modern landmark, designed by French architect Jean Nouvel and topped with a vast flying saucer-shaped dome comprising an impossibly intricate tangle of metal latticework – the whole thing weighs around 7,500 tons, roughly the same as the Eiffel Tower. Inside, galleries house around 600 items from the museum's permanent collection (alongside a constantly changing selection of loan exhibits) showcasing cultures from around the world stretching from pre-history to the twentieth century and with highlights ranging from Bellini's serene *Virgin and Child* (1485) to a strikingly abstract indigo-and-gold folio from the ninth-century Tunisian "Blue Quran".

Sheikh Zayed Mosque

Sheikh Zayed Mosque

MAP P.92

15km (9 miles) from central Abu Dhabi, between Al Ain and Al Khaleej al Arabi roads, ⓦ szgmc.gov.ae.

The mighty **Sheikh Zayed Mosque** dominates all landward approaches to the city. Completed in 2007, it's one of the world's biggest – and certainly the most expensive, having taken twelve years to build at a cost of around $500 million. It's also unusual in being one of the few mosques in the UAE **open to non-Muslims**.

The huge **exterior** is framed by four 107m-high (351ft) minarets and topped with some eighty domes. Entrance to the mosque is through a vast **courtyard** – capable of accommodating some 40,000 worshippers. Flanking one side is the vast **prayer hall**, home to the world's largest carpet and biggest chandelier, although it's the extraordinary muted opulence of the design that impresses, with every surface richly carved and decorated. Free guided tours run regularly throughout the day (no booking required).

Yas Island

MAP P.92

About 30–35km (18–22 miles) from central Abu Dhabi; access either from the Dubai highway or along the road via Saadiyat Island.

On the outermost edges of the city, **Yas Island** is home to the **Yas Marina Circuit** (ⓦ yasmarinacircuit.com), which hosts the annual Abu Dhabi F1 Grand Prix. If you fancy a bit of Formula 1 action yourself, head to the jaw-droppingly huge **Ferrari World** (ⓦ ferrariworldabudhabi.com) theme park just down the road, offering a range of rides.

Cafés

Emirates Palace Afternoon Tea

MAP P.92
Emirates Palace Hotel, Corniche Rd West
emiratespalace.com.
The *Emirates Palace*'s beautiful foyer café makes a memorable setting for one of the Middle East's most sumptuous afternoon teas, mixing Arabian-inspired delicacies and French pastries (485dh per couple). Prior online reservations essential although the website is confusing – search for "Emirates Palace afternoon tea" if all else fails. DhDhDhDh

Lebanese Mill

MAP P.92
Najda St 02 671 2277.
This shoebox café serves up a memorable slice of local life, attracting a lively mix of expat Arabs, Emiratis and tourists thanks to its more-ish mezze, sandwiches, shwarmas and grills, served in generous portions and at cut-throat prices. Often packed so don't be surprised if you have to wait for a table. Dh

Tarbouche

MAP P.92
Souk, World Trade Center
02 628 2220.
Convenient lunchtime pitstop beautifully located in the stunning central atrium of the World Trade Center Souk, with a decent selection of mainstream Middle Eastern offerings (mezze from around 20dh, grills from 45dh), plus sandwiches and salads. DhDh

Restaurants

Finz

MAP P.92
Beach Rotana Hotel, 10th St, Tourist Club Area, rotana.com/beachrotana.
One of the best seafood restaurants in town, occupying an unusual A-frame wooden dining room and terrace with superb views of Al Maryah Island. The menu features a wide selection of fish and seafood cooked to perfection – moules marinière, Canadian live lobster, Mediterranean sea bass and so on. DhDhDh

India Palace

MAP P.92
As Salam St, Tourist Club Area,
indiapalace.ae.
Long-established and pleasantly old-fashioned Indian restaurant, serving up a big spread of tasty and very reasonably priced North Indian meat, seafood and veg offerings. DhDh.

Stratos

MAP P.92
Le Royal Méridien hotel, Sheikh Khalifa St
stratosabudhabi.com.
Bird's-eye city views are the main attraction at this revolving lounge bar and restaurant. The modern European-style food isn't bad either, comprising a nice mix of seafood starters and Josper-cooked meat mains. Alternatively, just come for a drink. DhDhDhDh

Bar

Brauhaus

MAP P.92
Beach Rotana Hotel, 10th St, Tourist Club Area, rotana.com/beachrotana.
This convivial pub-cum-restaurant makes a surprisingly convincing stab at an authentic Bavarian *bierkeller*, with speciality German beers on tap or by the bottle and a good range of food to soak it all up with, served to the accompaniment of Bavarian marching bands and other Teutonic sounds. Very popular, so arrive early if you want to bag a seat.

ACCOMMODATION

Burj al Arab

Accommodation

Dubai has a vast range of accommodation, much of it aimed at big spenders. At the top end of the market, the city has some of the most stunning – and expensive – hotels on the planet, from the futuristic *Burj al Arab* – the world's first "seven-star" hotel – to traditional Arabian-themed palaces such as *Al Qasr* and the *One&Only Royal Mirage*, and suave modern city hotels like *Raffles* and *Grosvenor House* – as well as the vast *Atlantis* mega-resort. There are plenty of mid-range options, although virtually all establishments in this price range tend towards the functional and characterless. There's no real budget accommodation in Dubai, and you won't find a double room anywhere in the city for much less than about 300dh ($80).

Bur Dubai

ARABIAN COURTYARD MAP P.26, POCKET MAP M12. **Al Fahidi St. Sharaf DG metro, arabiancourtyard.com.** In a brilliantly central location opposite the Dubai Museum, this attractive four-star is a distinct cut above the other mid-range places in Bur Dubai – and usually excellent value too. Decor features a nice mix of modern and Arabian styles, while facilities include a small gym and spa – though the pool is tiny. **DhDh**

BARJEEL HERITAGE GUEST HOUSE MAP P.26, POCKET MAP M10. **Shindagha waterfront. Al Ghubaiba metro 054 319 1286.** Located between Al Ghubaiba metro station and Sheikh Saeed al Maktoum House, this appealing heritage guesthouse occupies a fine old historic building in a picture-perfect location on the Shindagha waterfront. Rooms are arranged around a beautiful internal courtyard and attractively furnished in traditional Arabian style, and there's also a good restaurant attached. **DhDh**

FOUR POINTS SHERATON BUR DUBAI MAP P.26, POCKET MAP M13. **Khalid Bin al Waleed Rd. Sharaf DG metro, marriott.com/en-gb/hotels/travel/dxbfp-four-points-bur-dubai/.** Understated but comfortable four-star with nicely furnished rooms in simple international style and good facilities including a gym, (smallish) swimming pool, the excellent *Antique Bazaar* restaurant and the cosy *Viceroy Bar* (see page 33). **DhDh**

QUEEN ELIZABETH 2 MAP P.26, POCKET MAP L1. **Port Rashid. Al Ghubaiba metro.**

Accommodation price codes

Pricing (in UAE dirhams) is based on a two people sharing a standard double room for one night in high season including all government taxes and the daily tourism fee, but not including breakfast.

Dh	under 350dh
DhDh	350–750dh
DhDhDh	750–1500dh
DhDhDhDh	over 1500dh

Room rates

Hotels in all price ranges chop and change their room rates constantly according to the time of year and demand, so a hotel may be brilliant value one week, and a rip-off the next. The rates given in our reviews are a very rough guide to average prices in high season; actual costs may sometimes be a little lower or significantly higher depending on demand. Prices usually (but not always) depend on the **season**. In general, they're highest during the cool winter months from November to February and cheapest in high summer (June to August), when rates at some places can tumble by thirty percent or more. **Taxes** (a ten percent service charge, a ten percent municipality tax and a tourism fee of 7–20dh per day depending on the star rating of the accommodation) are sometimes included in the quoted rate, but not always, so check when booking or you might find yourself suddenly having to cough up an extra twenty percent. All the prices given in the reviews below are for the **cheapest double room in high season** (excluding Christmas and New Year), inclusive of all taxes.

Ⓦ qe2.com. Experience a real slice of maritime history with a stay aboard the iconic *Queen Elizabeth 2* ocean liner, retired from service in 2008 and now repurposed as a floating hotel at Bur Dubai's Port Rashid. The cabin rooms are, not surprisingly, on the small side, but have been very attractively refurbished, while on-board facilities include a couple of time-warped restaurants and the crusty old *Golden Lion* pub (see page 33). Rates are surprisingly affordable – although obviously it's the chance to take in the atmosphere of this famous ship that's the real draw. **DhDh**

TIME PALACE HOTEL MAP P.26, **POCKET MAP M11. Just off Al Fahidi St. Al Ghubaiba metro Ⓦ timepalacehotel.com.** The most consistently reliable budget hotel in Bur Dubai, with spacious and very well-maintained rooms in an unbeatable location just up from the main entrance to the Textile Souk. Tends to get booked up well in advance, so reserve early. **Dh**

XVA MAP P.26, **POCKET MAP N12. Bastakiya. Sharaf DG metro Ⓦ xvahotel.com.** Atmospheric hotel-cum-café (see page) tucked away around the back of a fine old Bastakiya house. Rooms are on the small side but brimming with character, featuring Arabian furnishings, slatted windows and four-poster beds, plus captivating views over the surrounding wind towers. Good value. **DhDh**

Deira

CROWNE PLAZA DUBAI DEIRA MAP **P.36, POCKET MAP P4. Salahuddin Rd. Salah al Din metro, Ⓦ crowneplaza.com.** One of Deira's oldest accommodation landmarks, formerly the *Renaissance Hotel*, now given a spruce modern makeover. The unfashionable address (although very handy for both airport and metro) and factory-like exterior don't immediately inspire, but the airy atrium and bigger-than-average rooms tick all the right boxes, while facilities include a health club, medium-sized pool, plus bar and a couple of restaurants. **DhDh**

GOLDEN SANDS HOTEL CREEK MAP **P.36, POCKET MAP N3. Baniyas Rd. Al Rigga metro, Ⓦ goldensandscreek.com/.** Deira's smartest hotel (formerly the Hilton Dubai Creek), with chrome-clad public areas and stylish, well-equipped rooms decorated in minimalist whites and creams; most also have grand Creek views. There's also a health club, a small rooftop pool and a couple of decent restaurants. **DhDhDh**

HYATT PLACE BANIYAS SQUARE MAP P.36, POCKET MAP O12. **Baniyas Square. Baniyas Square metro, ⓦ dubaibaniyassquare.place.hyatt.com.** In an excellently central location overlooking Baniyas Square, this smart new Hyatt offers quality but relatively affordable accommodation with five-star comforts but without all the trappings of a big hotel. The spacious rooms come with floor-to-ceiling windows (and good views over the square from some) and cool decor, while facilities include a restaurant, coffee-lounge-cum-bar and a small pool. **DhDh**

PREMIER INN DUBAI INTERNATIONAL AIRPORT MAP P.36, POCKET MAP O8. **Airport, opposite Terminal 3. Airport Terminal 3 metro, ⓦ premierinn.com.** Rooms are functional and the location isn't particularly atmospheric (unless you like airports – although rooms are well soundproofed so plane noise shouldn't be a problem). On the upside you're only a short metro ride away from the old city and you probably won't find a cheaper room in town – plus, needless to say, it's super-convenient when flying in or out. Facilities include restaurant, bar and a small pool. **Dh**

RADISSON BLU DUBAI DEIRA CREEK MAP P.36, POCKET MAP O13. **Baniyas Rd. Union metro, ⓦ radissonblu.com.** The oldest five-star in the city, this *grande dame* of a hotel still has plenty going for it: an extremely central location, a great spread of restaurants and bars and a scenic position right on the Creek, of which all rooms have a view. **DhDhDh**

SHERATON DUBAI CREEK MAP P.36, POCKET MAP N3. **Baniyas Rd. Union metro, ⓦ sheraton.com/dubai.** This old-fashioned five-star enjoys a scenic Creekside setting and opulent public areas with lots of shiny white marble. Roughly half the rooms have Creek views (the higher the better) and facilities include a small pool plus good in-house restaurants, including the excellent *Vivaldi* (see page 39) and the homely Chelsea Arms Pub, one of the city's oldest bars. **DhDh**

The inner suburbs

ARABIAN PARK DUBAI MAP P.44, POCKET MAP K7. **Al Jadaf St, Jaddaf. Al Jadaf metro, ⓦ rotana.com.** This functional three-star is currently one of Dubai's best deals. The location feels a bit middle-of-nowhere but is only a 500m (1640ft) walk to the metro, from where it's just three stops to the old city centre. Rooms are comfortably bland and there's a small pool plus restaurant, while the in-house *Cheers* bar serves some of the cheapest pints in the city. **Dh**

GRAND HYATT MAP P.44, POCKET MAP I7. **Sheikh Rashid Rd, Oud Metha. Dubai Healthcare City metro, ⓦ dubai.grand.hyatt.com.** This colossus of a hotel is grand in every sense – the vast atrium alone could easily swallow two or three smaller establishments, while facilities include four pools, spa, kids' club, gym, thirteen restaurants and bars, and beautiful, spacious grounds. The only real drawback is its middle-of-nowhere location, although it is conveniently close to the metro and major roads. **DhDhDh**

PARK HYATT MAP P.44, POCKET MAP N6. **Dubai Creek Golf and Yacht Club, Garhoud. Deira City Centre metro, ⓦ dubai.park.hyatt.com.** Alluring five-star set in a beautiful complex of quasi-Moroccan-style buildings surrounded by extensive grounds with plenty of palm trees. Rooms (some with fine Creek views) are unusually large, while facilities include a big pool and the superb Amara spa, plus the *Thai Kitchen* restaurant and attractive *The Pool* bar (see page 49). **DhDhDhDh**

RAFFLES MAP P.44, POCKET MAP I6. **Sheikh Rashid Rd, Oud Metha. Dubai Healthcare City metro, ⓦ raffles.com/dubai.** Vying with the *Park Hyatt* for the title of Dubai's finest city-centre hotel, the spectacular *Raffles* is designed in the form of an enormous postmodern pyramid, with a beautifully executed blend of Egyptian and Asian styling. Rooms feature silky-smooth contemporary decor and fine city views, while facilities include a good selection of eating and drinking establishments, a big pool and extensive grounds. **DhDhDhDh**

Sheikh Zayed Road and Downtown Dubai

ARMANI HOTEL MAP P.52, POCKET MAP E4. **Floors 5–8 & 38–39, Burj Khalifa. Burj Khalifa/Dubai Mall metro, ⓦ armanihotels.com.** Located in the iconic Burj Khalifa, this was the world's first Armani hotel when it opened in 2010. The whole place is kitted out in furnishings from Giorgio's Casa Armani homeware range – all muted whites, greys, browns and blacks. Facilities include a string of fine eating and drinking venues (see page 56), a cool spa and pool. **DhDhDhDh**

DUSIT THANI MAP P.52, POCKET MAP F4. **Sheikh Zayed Rd. Financial Centre metro, ⓦ dusit.com.** Thai-owned and -styled five-star combining serene interior design and ultra-attentive service. Rooms are stylishly decorated in soothing creams and browns, while facilities include the excellent *Benjarong* restaurant (see page 57). **DhDhDh**

IBIS WORLD TRADE CENTRE MAP P.52, POCKET MAP H4. **Sheikh Zayed Rd. World Trade Centre metro, ⓦ accorhotels.com.** The cheapest lodgings in this part of town. Rooms are small but comfortable (with nice views from higher ones), and guests can use the fitness centre and pools at the adjacent *Novotel* for a small fee. **DhDh**

JUMEIRAH EMIRATES TOWERS MAP P.52, POCKET MAP G4. **Sheikh Zayed Rd. Emirates Towers metro, ⓦ jumeirahemiratestowers.com.** Occupying the smaller of the two iconic Emirates Towers, this exclusive establishment is generally rated the top business hotel in the city, catering mainly to senior execs on expense accounts. Rooms appear designed to calm the nerves of stressed-out CEOs, with muted colours and soothingly understated furnishings, and there's also a dedicated ladies' floor, plus a good-sized pool and health club. **DhDhDhDh**

MANZIL DOWNTOWN DUBAI MAP P.52, POCKET MAP E5. **Sheikh Mohammed bin Rashid Blvd (Emaar Blvd), Old Town. Burj Khalifa/Dubai Mall metro, ⓦ vida-hotels.com.** Stylish little hotel with an attractive mix of contemporary and traditional Arabian styling. Rooms are on the small side, although there's a decent spread of amenities including a reasonable-sized pool and the attractive *Courtyard* restaurant (see page 57). The nearby *Vida Downtown Dubai* hotel, run by the same company, is very similar. **DhDhDh**

THE PALACE MAP P.52, POCKET MAP E5. **Sheikh Mohammed bin Rashid Blvd (Emaar Blvd), Old Town. Burj Khalifa/Dubai Mall metro, ⓦ addresshotels.com.** Opulent, Arabian-themed "city-resort" with lavish, quasi-Moroccan styling and a perfect lakeside view of the Dubai Fountain and Burj, best enjoyed from the fine in-house *Thiptara* restaurant (see page 58). Facilities include a superb spa and large lakeside pool. **DhDhDhDh**

SHANGRI-LA MAP P.52, POCKET MAP F4. **Sheikh Zayed Rd. Financial Centre metro, ⓦ shangri-la.com.** The most stylish hotel on Sheikh Zayed Rd, the *Shangri-La* is pure contemporary class – a beguiling mix of Zen-chic and Scandinavian-cool. Rooms come with smooth pine finishes, beautiful artworks and mirrors everywhere, while leisure facilities include one of the biggest pools in this part of town plus several excellent restaurants, including the seductive *Hoi An* (see page 57). **DhDhDh**

TOWERS ROTANA MAP P.52, POCKET MAP G3. **Sheikh Zayed Rd. Financial Centre metro, ⓦ rotana.com.** This shiny four-star is usually one of the cheapest Shekih Zayed Rd options – a bit run-of-the-mill compared to other nearby places but with comfortable rooms and amenities including a couple of decent in-house restaurants and the ever-popular *Long's Bar* (see page 59). **DhDhDh**

Jumeirah

DUBAI MARINE BEACH RESORT MAP P.61, POCKET MAP H1. **Jumeirah Rd, near Jumeirah Mosque, ⓦ dxbmarine.com.** This pocket-sized resort is the only five-star in Dubai where you can be on the beach but also within easy striking distance of the old city. The central location means that beach and grounds don't compare with places further south, although the resort scores highly for its lively collection of bars and clubs, and turns into a bit of a party palace after dark. **DhDhDh**

The Burj al Arab and around

BURJ AL ARAB MAP P.66, POCKET MAP K15. **Ⓦ burj-al-arab.com.** A stay in this staggering hotel (see page 64) is the ultimate Dubaian luxury. The "seven-star" facilities include fabulous split-level deluxe suites (the lowest category of accommodation – there are no ordinary rooms here), arrival in a chauffeur-driven Rolls and your own butler, access to the superlative Assawan Spa, a handful of spectacular restaurants and bars, and a fabulous stretch of beach. **DhDhDhDh**

DAR AL MASYAF MAP P.66, POCKET MAP J16. **Madinat Jumeirah, Ⓦ madinatjumeirah.com.** A more intimate and upmarket alternative to the Madinat Jumeirah's bigger hotels (there are now three following the opening of Naseem), *Dar al Masyaf* consists of a chain of modest, low-rise private villas scattered around the edges of the Madinat complex within extensive, palm-studded gardens. Each villa contains a small number of rooms, sharing an exclusive pool and decorated in the deluxe Arabian manner of *Al Qasr* and *Mina A'Salam*, whose myriad facilities they share. **DhDhDhDh**

IBIS DUBAI MALL OF THE EMIRATES MAP P.66, POCKET MAP J18. **2A St, near the Mall of the Emirates. Mall of the Emirates metro, Ⓦ ibishotel.com.** This cheery little no-frills hotel is usually one of the cheaper options in southern Dubai, with good-value rooms and a decent location on the south side of the Mall of the Emirates. **DhDh**

JUMEIRAH BEACH HOTEL MAP P.66, POCKET MAP L15. **Jumeirah Rd, Ⓦ jumeirah.com.** Famous old Dubai landmark (see page 65), and still an excellent place to stay, with a vast range of facilities including around twenty restaurants, five pools, diving centre – plus jaw-dropping views of the adjacent Burj al Arab. It's particularly good for families, with kids' club, spacious grounds and a fine stretch of beach with plenty of watersports available; guests also get unlimited access to Wild Wadi next door. **DhDhDhDh**

MINA A'SALAM MAP P.66, POCKET MAP K15. **Madinat Jumeirah, Ⓦ madinatjumeirah.com.** Part of the stunning Madinat Jumeirah complex, *Mina A'Salam* ("Harbour of Peace") shares the Madinat's styling, with beautifully furnished rooms featuring traditional Arabian wooden furniture and fabrics. Facilities include a nice-looking stretch of private beach, three pools plus the forty-odd restaurants, bars and myriad shops of the adjacent souk complex. **DhDhDhDh**

AL QASR MAP P.66, POCKET MAP K16. **Madinat Jumeirah, Ⓦ madinatjumeirah.com.** This extravagant Arabian-themed hotel looks like something out of a film set, from the opulent public areas to the swanky rooms with show-stopping views, sumptuous decor and pretty much every luxury and mod con you can imagine. There's also a huge pool and all the facilities of the Madinat Jumeirah on your doorstep. **DhDhDhDh**

The Palm Jumeirah and Dubai Marina

THE ADDRESS DUBAI MARINA MAP P.74, POCKET MAP B16. **Dubai Marina. Sohba Realty metro, Ⓦ theaddress.com.** The best of the non-beachfront hotels in this part of town, right next to the Marina Mall and as smooth as you like, with outstanding service and soothing decor in muted creams and browns. Rooms come with all mod cons, while those on higher floors have terrific views. Facilities include a smart 24hr gym and a huge ovoid pool – the biggest in the Marina. **DhDhDhDh**

ATLANTIS, THE PALM MAP P.74, POCKET MAP E10. **Palm Jumeirah. Palm Atlantis monorail, Ⓦ atlantis.com.** This vast mega-resort (see page 73) is the exact opposite of tasteful, but can't be beaten when it comes to in-house attractions, including a water park, dolphinarium, celebrity-chef restaurants, kicking bars and clubs, luxurious spa and vast swathes of sand. There are also excellent kids' facilities, making it a good place for a (very pricey) family holiday, with everything you need under one very large roof, while staying here also gets you free or discounted admission to the otherwise expensive on-site activities. It's not the most peaceful place in town, however, more suited to an up-tempo family holiday than a romantic break. **DhDhDhDh**

GROSVENOR HOUSE MAP P.74, POCKET MAP C16. **Al Sufouh Rd. Sobha Realty metro, ⓦ grosvenorhouse-dubai.com.** One of Dubai's smoothest hotels, set slightly away from the seafront in a pair of elegantly tapering skyscrapers. The entire hotel is a model of contemporary cool, from the suave public areas right through to the elegantly furnished rooms. Facilities include a pool, two excellent spas, and one of the city's best selections of restaurants and bars (see page 78), while guests also have free use of the beach and facilities at the nearby *Le Royal Méridien*. **DhDhDhDh**

HILTON DUBAI JUMEIRAH MAP P.74, POCKET MAP B15. **The Walk at Jumeirah Beach Residence. Jumeirah Beach Residence 1 tram station, ⓦ hilton.com.** Glitzy Hilton boasts lots of shiny metal and carries an air of cosmopolitan chic – more of a city-slicker's beach bolt-hole than family seaside resort. Rooms are bright and cheerfully decorated, although facilities are relatively limited compared to nearby places. Outside there's a medium-sized pool and lovely (though rather small) terraced gardens running down to the sea. **DhDhDh**

JANNAH PLACE DUBAI MARINA MAP P.74, POCKET MAP A16. **Nasaq St, Marina Promenade. Sobha Realty metro,** ⓦ www.jannah-hotels.com. A rare budget option in this part of town, these fully serviced studios and two-bedroom apartments (all with kitchen and washing machine) offer an excellent city pied-a-terre in a great location close to the Marina. **DhDh**

JUMEIRAH ZABEEL SARAY MAP P.74, POCKET MAP C13. **West Crescent, Palm Jumeirah, ⓦ jumeirah.com.** One of Dubai's most entertainingly extravagant hotels: relatively understated from outside, but a riot of quirky opulence within. Public areas and rooms are designed in lavish quasi-Ottoman style, while the hotel's spectacular array of bars and restaurants ranges through a whole encyclopedia of styles – fake Rajasthani palace, faux French chateau, burlesque music hall and Eskimo spaceship – all beautifully done, and good fun besides. Facilities include the vast Talisse Ottoman Spa and in-house cinema, while outside there are beautiful grounds, a gorgeous infinity pool and extensive beach (with kids' club). **DhDhDhDh**

LE MÉRIDIEN MINA SEYAHI MAP P.74, POCKET MAP D15. **Al Sufouh Rd. Mina Seyahi tram station, ⓦ lemeridien-minaseyahi.com.** This venerable old five-star isn't much to look at and is one of Dubai's most dated big hotels, although it scores highly for its superb grounds and big swathe of beach, where you'll also find the kicking *Barasti* beachside bar (see page 80). **DhDhDh**

LE ROYAL MÉRIDIEN BEACH RESORT AND SPA MAP P.74, POCKET MAP C15. **The Walk at Jumeirah Beach Residence. Jumeirah Beach Residence 1 tram station, ⓦ leroyalmeridien-dubai.com.** This large and slightly overblown five-star lacks the style of other places along the beach although it compensates with its extensive grounds and beach, complete with three larger-than-average pools – excellent for families. Facilities include the ostentatious, Roman-themed Caracalla Spa and a good spread of restaurants, including the excellent *Rhodes Twenty10* (see page 79). Often excellent value. **DhDhDhDh**

ONE&ONLY THE PALM MAP P.74, POCKET MAP C14. **West Crescent, Palm Jumeirah, ⓦ thepalm.oneandonlyresorts.com.** A haven of intimate, understated luxury amid the burgeoning mega-resorts sprouting up around the Palm in an ever-increasing string of bling, *One&Only The Palm* is small, peaceful and very civilized (apart from the terrifying price tag). The style is quasi-Moorish, with hints of the Alhambra in Granada, and neat gardens lining a gorgeous pool, and there's also a fine spa and almost 500m (1640ft) of private beach. A boat shuttle runs guests over to the mainland from the hotel's own marina, where you'll also find the attractive waterside *101* bar-restaurant (see page 80). **DhDhDhDh**

ONE&ONLY ROYAL MIRAGE MAP P.74, POCKET MAP E15. **Al Sufouh Rd. Media City/Palm Jumeirah tram stations, ⓦ royalmirage.oneandonlyresorts.com.** The most romantic hotel in town, this dreamy resort is the perfect *One Thousand and One Nights* fantasy made flesh, with a superb sequence of quasi-Moroccan-style buildings scattered amid extensive, palm-filled grounds. The whole complex is actually three hotels in one: *The Palace*, the *Arabian Court* and the *Residence & Spa*, each a little bit more sumptuous (and expensive) than the last. Rooms feature Arabian decor, reproduction antique wooden furniture and colourful rugs, while facilities include a 1km (0.6 miles) stretch of private beach, four pools, the delectable hammam-style spa and some of the best restaurants and bars in town (see page 78) – all at sometimes surprisingly affordable rates. **DhDhDhDh**

RITZ-CARLTON MAP P.74, POCKET MAP B15. **The Walk at Jumeirah Beach Residence. Jumeirah Beach Residence 1 tram station, ⓦ ritzcarlton.com.** Set in a low-rise, Tuscan-style ochre building, this very stylish establishment is one of the classiest in the city. Rooms are spacious, with slightly chintzy decor, while public areas boast all the charm of a luxurious old country house, especially in the sumptuous lobby lounge. There's also a big and very quiet stretch of private beach and gardens, an attractive spa and good kids' facilities. **DhDhDhDh**

SHERATON JUMEIRAH BEACH MAP P.74, POCKET MAP A15. **The Walk at Jumeirah Beach Residence. Jumeirah Beach Residence 2 tram station, ⓦ sheraton.com/jumeirahbeach.** The area's oldest and most low-key five-star, particularly good for families, with extensive palm-studded gardens and beach and a watersports centre, while kids get their own pool area, playground and day-care club. Usually a bit cheaper than the nearby competition, although no bargain. **DhDhDh**

Out of the city

AL AIN ROTANA MAP P.88. **120th Street, ⓦ rotana.com/alainrotana.** This long-running five-star is easily the best of the city's rather limited selection of hotels, and conveniently close to the city centre as well. Rooms are large and well-appointed, and there are also spacious gardens complete with a pair of pools and a couple of good in-house restaurants, including the fun *Min Zaman* (see page 89). **DhDh**

BAB AL SHAMS DESERT RESORT AND SPA POCKET MAP E9, **ⓦ babalshams.com.** Hidden out in the desert a 45min drive from the airport, this gorgeous resort occupies a wonderfully atmospheric replica Arabian fort, with desert camel- and horseriding or falconry displays the order of the day, rather than lounging on the beach. Rooms are decorated in traditional Gulf style, with rustic ochre walls and Bedouin-style fabrics, while facilities include a magnificent infinity pool and a good selection of restaurants. **DhDhDh**

DESERT PALM **Inside front cover flap.** POCKET MAP G9, **ⓦ melia.com.** On the edge of Dubai, around a 20min drive from the city centre, the *Desert Palm* is a pleasantly laidback suburban bolt-hole, surrounded by polo fields, with distant views of the skyscrapers along Sheikh Zayed Rd. Rooms are beautifully designed and equipped with fancy mod-cons, while facilities include the superb in-house Samana Spa. **DhDhDh**

AL MAHA DESERT RESORT AND SPA **MAP P.88. Dubai Desert Conservation Reserve, Al Ain Rd, ⓦ al-maha.com.** Some 60km (37 miles) from Dubai, this very exclusive, very expensive resort occupies a picture-perfect setting amid the pristine Dubai Desert Conservation Reserve (see page 89) – gazelles and rare Arabian oryx can often been seen wandering through the grounds. The resort is styled like a Bedouin encampment, with accommodation in tented suites featuring handcrafted furnishings and artefacts plus small private pools, and stunning views of the surrounding dunes. Activities include falconry, camel treks, horseriding, archery, 4WD desert drives and guided nature walks – or just relax in the resort's serene spa. Full board (including two desert activities per day) around **DhDhDhDh**

Abu Dhabi

BEACH ROTANA MAP P.92. **10th St, Al Zahiyah, ⓦ rotana.com/beachrotana.** Smart modern resort-style hotel in the so-called Tourist Club Area, one of Abu Dhabi downtown's liveliest districts. Rooms are spacious and attractively styled, and there's a nice stretch of waterfront beach and gardens, plus an excellent spread of places to eat and drink. **DhDh**

CONRAD ABU DHABI ETIHAD TOWERS MAP P.92. **Etihad Towers, Corniche Rd West, ⓦ hilton.com/en/hotels/auhetci-conrad-abu-dhabi-etihad-towers/.** Swanky hotel occupying one of the five futuristic skyscrapers of the landmark Etihad Towers development – a cutting-edge alternative to the staid *Emirates Palace* opposite. Rooms are large, luxurious and full of state-of-the-art mod cons, while facilities include three pools, private beach and a serene spa. **DhDhDh**

EMIRATES PALACE MAP P.92. **Corniche Rd West, ⓦ emiratespalace.com.** Abu Dhabi's landmark hotel (see page 90) is the favoured residence of visiting heads of state and assorted celebrities, with every luxury you could think of, including lots of swanky restaurants and a vast swathe of beach. Rates aren't always as crushingly expensive as you might expect – check the website for offers. **DhDhDhDh**

INTERCONTINENTAL MAP P.92. **Al Bateen St, Al Bateen, ⓦ ihg.com.** One of the oldest five-stars in Abu Dhabi, and still among the best, set in an attractive coastal location on the quiet southern side of the centre with views of the nearby Etihad Towers and *Emirates Palace* beyond. Renovations have kept rooms in tiptop condition, while the excellent facilities include a huge pool, well-equipped gym, one of the city's best selections of restaurants and bars, and a fine swathe of beautiful white sand. **DhDhDh**

ROYAL ROSE HOTEL MAP P.92. **1025 Sheikh Zayed the 1st St, Al Markaziyah, ⓦ royalrosehotel.com.** The bizarre French-chateau-on-steroids architecture is pretty horrible and the interior design is like a festival of chintz – although rates are super competitive and the central location is just about perfect. **DhDh**

SHANGRI-LA MAP P.92. **Qaryat al Beri, ⓦ shangri-la.com/abudhabi.** One of the city's most alluring hotels, with gorgeous Arabian Nights decor, huge gardens, four pools, the lovely Chi spa, a gorgeous infinity pool which appears to flow straight into the sea, and wonderful views of the Sheikh Zayed Mosque. Surprisingly affordable, given the standard. **DhDhDh**

ESSENTIALS

Highway intersection and the Dubai Metro

Arrival

Unless you're travelling overland from neighbouring Oman or sailing in on a cruise ship, you'll almost certainly arrive at Dubai's sparkling international **airport (DXB)** close to the old city centre – although a handful of flights land at the new Al Maktoum International Airport (DWC) in the far south of the city.

The airport (ⓦ dubaiairports.ae) is very centrally located in the district of Garhoud, around 7km (4.5 miles) from the city centre. There are three passenger terminals: Terminal 1 is where most international flights arrive; Terminal 3 is where all Emirates airlines flights land; and Terminal 2 is used by smaller regional carriers. All three terminals have plenty of ATMs, currency exchange booths and car-rental outlets (see page 111).

Both Terminal 1 and Terminal 3 have dedicated **metro stations**, offering quick and inexpensive transport into the city and there are also various airport **buses,** although these are of only limited use for most visitors. Note that for both metro and buses you'll have to buy a Nol card or ticket (see page 109) before boarding. Alternatively, there are plentiful **taxis** (although note that they charge a 25dh flag fare when picking up from the airport, rather than the usual 12dh).

Getting around

Dubai is very spread out – it's around 25km (15.5 miles) from the city centre down to Dubai Marina – but getting around is relatively straightforward and inexpensive, thanks mainly to the excellent metro system. Taxis are also plentiful while there are also buses and boats, as well as cheap car rental. Full information about the city's public transport is available on the Roads & Transport Authority (RTA) website at ⓦ rta.ae. The RTA also provide the useful **online "Wojhati" travel planner and a handy app**.

By metro

The **Dubai Metro** (ⓦ rta.ae) offers a cheap, fast and convenient way of getting around, with state-of-the-art driverless trains and eye-catching modern stations. It consists of two lines: the 67km-long (42 miles) **Red Line**, running from Centrepoint, near the airport, down Sheikh Zayed Road to UAE Exchange in the far south of the city (plus a branch line to the Expo 2020 site); and the 22km-long (14 miles) **Green Line**, which arcs around the city centre, running from Etisalat, north of the airport, via Deira and Bur Dubai and then down to the Creek at Jaddaf. **Trains** run roughly every five to nine minutes, with services running Monday to Saturday from around 5am to around midnight (until 1am on Fri), and on Sundays from 8am to 1am. Note that the **names** of metro stations are commercially sponsored and change with maddening regularity, so don't be surprised if the same station is referred to by two or more different names (Sobha Realty station on the Red Line, for example, which opened in 2010 under the name Dubai Marina station and was then rechristened DAMAC Properties in 2014 before acquiring its latest moniker in 2020). All trains have a dedicated carriage for **women and children** (look for the signs above the platform barriers) plus a **Gold Class** compartment at the front of/back of the train – these have slightly plusher seating and decor, although the main benefit is that they're usually fairly empty, meaning that you're pretty much guaranteed a

Nol cards

Almost all Dubai's public transport services – **metro**, **trams, buses** and some **boats** (but not abras) – are covered by the **Nol** system (rta.ae). To use any of these forms of transport you'll need to buy a prepaid Nol card or ticket ahead of travel; no tickets are sold on board the relevant trains, trams, buses or boats. Cards can be **bought** and **topped up** at any metro station or at one of the machines located at 64 bus stops around the city.

Fares are based on how many of Dubai's seven travel zones you pass through, ranging from 4dh up to a maximum of 8.50dh for a single trip (8dh–17dh in Gold Class).

There are two main types of Nol card; all are valid for five years and can store up to 1000dh worth of credit. The **Silver Card** costs 25dh (including 19dh credit). The **Gold Card** (same price) is almost identical but allows users to travel on Gold Class compartments on the metro.

An alternative is the **Red Ticket** (a paper ticket, rather than a card). This has been specifically designed for tourists, costs just 2dh and is valid for 90 days. The main benefit of the Red Ticket is that it allows you to purchase a useful one-day pass (22/44dh in regular/Gold class) valid citywide, although you'll have to recharge the ticket for each day of travel (with a maximum of five recharges).

seat, something you'll often struggle to find in ordinary carriages.

Fares are calculated according to the Nol card system, which also covers the city's buses, trams and some boat services.

By tram

The **Dubai Tram** offers a convenient (if not desperately fast) way of getting around the Marina and north towards Umm Suqeim. The tram links seamlessly with the metro (with interconnecting stations at DMCC and Sobha Realty) and also the **Palm Monorail** (see page 73). As on the metro, **fares** are covered by the Nol system (see above) and all trams have Gold Class and women-and-children-only carriages. Operating hours are Monday to Saturday 6am–1am and Sunday 9am–1am, with departures every eight minutes.

By taxi

Away from areas served by the metro and tram, the only way of getting around Dubai quickly is by **taxi**. There are usually plenty of cabs around at all times of day and night (except in Bur Dubai and Deira during the morning and evening rush hours and after dark). **Fares** are pretty good value: there's a minimum charge of 12dh per ride plus 1.82dh per kilometre. The exception is for taxis picked up from the airport, where a 25dh flag fare is imposed; there's also a 20dh surcharge if you take a taxi into Sharjah. You'll also have to pay a 4dh surcharge if your taxi travels through one of Dubai's four tollgates. **Tips** aren't strictly necessary but will be appreciated, and many taxi drivers will automatically keep the small change from fares unless you specifically ask for it back.

Taxis will generally accept routes across all of the emirates and are run by a number of different firms (Cars Taxi, Dubai Taxi and National Taxis are the largest). Taxis operated by all companies can be booked on 8008 8088 or via the DTC (Dubai Taxi Corporation) app.

By abra and waterbus

For all Dubai's sleek modern transport infrastructure, the easiest way of **crossing the Creek** is still by hopping aboard one of the quaint little wooden boats – or **abras** – which ferry passengers between Deira and Bur Dubai.

There are two main abra **routes**: from Deira Old Souk Abra Station to Bur Dubai Abra Station, and (slightly further down the Creek) from Al Sabkha Abra Station to Bur Dubai Old Souk Abra Station. The **fare** is just 1dh (under 5s free). Boats leave as soon as full (meaning, in practice, every couple of minutes), and the crossing takes about five minutes. Abras run from 6am to midnight, and 24hr on the route from Bur Dubai Old Souk to Al Sabkha.

An alternative to the traditional abra is the slightly fancier and more comfortable "**petrol heritage abra**" (as it's inelegantly described). Trips cost 2dh and boats run the two routes above along with two additional routes further south along the Creek connecting Al Fahidi and Al Seef on the Bur Dubai side with Baniyas in Deira.

Down in Dubai Marina, more modern **air-conditioned abras** (aka waterbuses) also connect Marina Mall and Marina Walk (daily noon to 11pm, Fri–Sun until midnight; 5dh), while additional evening services (daily 4–11.30pm) crisscross the Dubai Marina, with stops at Marina Mall, Marina Walk, Marina Promenade and Bluewaters Island (3dh, or 11dh to Bluewaters).

By ferry

Further memorable views of Dubai from the water can be had by taking a ride on the smart, modern Dubai Ferry. Services run between Al Ghubaiba in Bur Dubai and Dubai Marina, sailing around the outside of the Palm en route and with stops at the entrance to the Dubai Canal in Jumeirah and at Bluewaters Island and Marina Mall in the Marina itself. There are currently two services daily in each direction, leaving early afternoon and early evening and costing 50dh; the journey from Bur Dubai to the Marina takes around 2hr. There's also a twice-daily sightseeing round trip (75dh) from the Marina to the *Atlantis* resort on the Palm (although the boat doesn't actually stop at *Atlantis*). Check latest details at ⓦrta.ae, since tours and timings change frequently.

By bus

Dubai has a well-developed and efficient network of bus services, though it's of limited use for tourists with the possible exception of coastal services through Jumeirah, which refresh parts of the city the metro doesn't reach. Most services originate or terminate at either the **Gold Souk Bus Station** in Deira or **Al Ghubaiba Bus Station** in Bur Dubai (many services call at both). Stops elsewhere are clearly signed. Buses are included in the **Nol ticket scheme**, meaning that you'll need to be in possession of a paid-up Nol card or ticket (see page 109) before you get on the bus; tickets aren't sold on board.

Buses to **Sharjah** leave from Al Ghubaiba Bus Station, and also from Al Sabkha Bus Station in the middle of Deira (24hr; departures roughly every 20min from each station; 45min–1hr; 12dh). Buses to **Abu Dhabi** leave from Al Ghubaiba (daily 5am–11.30pm every 20min; 2hr–2hr 30min; 25dh) and from Ibn Battuta metro station (daily from 5am–1am; every 20min; 1hr 30min–2hr; 30dh). Minibuses to **Al Ain** leave from Al Ghubaiba (every 40min from 5.40pm to 10pm; 25dh). Nol cards can be used on some Sharjah and Abu Dhabi buses (but not on Al Ain services), or just buy a ticket at the bus station.

By car

Renting a car is another option but comes with a couple of caveats. Driving in Dubai isn't for the faint-hearted: the city's roads are permanently busy and standards of driving wayward and many people drive fast. However, for longer stays it will be useful to have your own transportation. **Navigational difficulties** are another big problem, given the city's ever-evolving layout.

For **car rental** contact any of the following: Avis (ⓦ avis.ae); Budget (ⓦ budget-uae.com); Europcar (ⓦ europcardubai.com); Hertz (ⓦ hertz.ae); Sixt (ⓦ sixt.ae); Thrifty (ⓦ thriftyuae.com).

Tours

Dubai has dozens of identikit tour operators who pull in a regular supply of punters in search of the instant "Arabian" experience. The emphasis is firmly on stereotypical **desert safaris** and touristy dhow **dinner cruises**, although a few operators offer more unusual activities ranging from falconry displays to desert hikes. **Prices** can vary quite considerably from operator to operator, so it's worth shopping around, although you generally get what you pay for, and some of the cheaper operators cut more corners than you might be comfortable with.

City tours

Generic city tours are offered by all the general tour operators in the box to follow. For more original insights, contact the **Sheikh Mohammed Centre for Cultural Understanding** in Bastakiya (ⓣ 04 353 6666, ⓦ cultures.ae) which runs interesting tours of Jumeirah Mosque and Bastakiya, along with other cultural events (see page 25).

If you've got the cash you might consider a helicopter tour of the city, offering peerless views of the Creek and coast. Trips can be arranged through numerous operators including soundalikes Helicopter Tour Dubai (ⓦ helicoptertourdubai.com) and Dubai Helicopter Tour (ⓦ www.helicoptertour.ae). Prices start from 710dh for twelve minutes.

Boat cruises

A more leisurely alternative to the standard Creek crossing by abra is to **charter your own boat** (120dh/hr per boat). Starting from the city centre, in an hour you can probably get down to the Dubai Creek Golf Club and back. To find an abra for rent, head to the nearest abra station and ask around. You can also hop in an abra outside the Dubai Mall for a short spin around the Dubai Fountain (daily 6–11.30pm; 68dh per person for 25min) and for sedate but pricey trips around the Madinat Jumeirah canals (ⓦ jumeirah.com; 100dh per person for 20min, or 650dh for two people with private hire).

Another option is to book one of the city's ever-popular after-dark **dinner cruises** (generally around 200–400dh per head), either along the Creek or (increasingly popular) in the Dubai Marina, while a couple of operators also run trips in the Dubai Water Canal. Most tours are in traditional replica wooden dhows, offering the chance to wine and dine on the water as your boat sails sedately up and between the souks or skyscrapers. Food tends to be a buffet for cheaper tours, à la carte for more upmarket options, and there's usually live onboard entertainment. Operators change with bewildering rapidity and most lack even a reliable website – the best approach is to search and book online using the latest reviews and any available discount deals.

Tour operators

Arabian Adventures ⓣ 800 272 2426, ⓦ arabian-adventures.com
Dubai Private Tour ⓣ 04 396 1444, ⓦ dubaiprivatetour.com
Funtours ⓣ 04 283 0889, ⓦ funtoursdubai.com
Knight Tours ⓣ 04 343 7725, ⓦ facebook.com/knighttoursdubai
Lama Tours ⓣ 04 297 3993, ⓦ lamadubai.com
Orient Tours ⓣ 04 282 8238, ⓦ orienttours.ae
Platinum Heritage Luxury Tours ⓣ 04 388 4044, ⓦ platinum-heritage.com
Travco ⓣ 04 336 6643, ⓦ travcotravel.ae

Desert safaris

One thing that virtually every visitor to Dubai does at some point is go on a **safari** to see some of the desert scenery surrounding Dubai. Although virtually all tours put the emphasis firmly on cheap thrills and touristy gimmicks, most people find the experience enjoyable, in a rather cheesy sort of way.

The vast majority of visitors opt for one of the endlessly popular **half-day safaris** (also known as "sunset safaris"). These are offered by every tour operator, and though the cost ranges from around 250dh up to 500dh – the more expensive tours generally offering superior service, better-quality food and a wider range of entertainment – the basic ingredients remain the same. Tours are in large 4WDs holding around eight passengers. You'll be picked up from your hotel between 3 and 4pm and then driven out into the desert. The usual destination is an area 45 minutes' drive out of town, opposite the massive dune popularly known as Big Red where you'll enjoy a spot of **dune-bashing** – driving at high speed up and down increasingly precipitous dunes amid great sprays of sand. You might also be given the chance to try your hand at a brief bit of **sand-skiing**. As dusk falls, you'll be driven off to one of the dozens of optimistically named desert "Bedouin camps" where attractions will typically include (very short) camel rides, henna painting, dressing up in Gulf national costume, and having your photo taken with an Emirati falcon perched on your arm. A passable international buffet dinner is then served, after which a belly dancer performs for another half-hour or so. The whole thing winds up at around 9.30pm, after which you'll be driven back to Dubai.

Directory

Accessible Travel

Dubai is probably the Middle East's most accessible destination for "People of Determination", as those with visual or mobility impairments are now officially described in the UAE. Most of the city's modern **hotels** now make at least some provision for guests with impaired mobility, and many of the city's four- and five-stars now have specially adapted rooms. Quite a few of the city's **malls** also have special facilities, including disabled parking spaces and specially equipped toilets. Inevitably, most of the city's older heritage buildings are not accessible (although the Dubai Museum is).

Transportation is fairly well set up. The **Dubai Metro** incorporates facilities to assist visually and mobility-impaired visitors, including tactile guide paths, lifts and ramps, as well as wheelchair spaces in all compartments, while **accessible taxis** can be booked on ☎ 800 88 088 or via the DTC (Dubai Taxi Corporation) app (but best to give a couple of hours' notice) equipped with ramps and lifts. There are also dedicated facilities at the **airport**.

Crime and drugs

Dubai is an exceptionally safe city – although a surprising number of tourists and expats manage to get themselves arrested for various breaches of local law. Violent crime is virtually unknown, and even instances of petty theft, pickpocketing and the like are relatively uncommon. The only time you're ever likely to be at risk is while driving. If you need to **call the police** in an emergency, dial ☎ 999.

You should not on any account attempt to enter (or even transit through) Dubai while in possession of any form of **illegal substance**. The death penalty is imposed for drug trafficking, and there's a mandatory four-year sentence for anyone caught in possession of drugs or other proscribed substances. It's vital to note that this doesn't just mean carrying drugs in a conventional sense, but also includes having an illegal substance in your **bloodstream or urine**, or being found in possession of even **microscopic amounts** of a banned substance, even if invisible to the naked eye. Note that poppy seeds (even in bakery products) are also banned. Dubai's hardline anti-drugs regime also extends to certain **prescription drugs**, including codeine and melatonin, which are also treated as illegal substances. If you're on any form of prescription medicine you're supposed to bring a doctor's letter and the original prescription from home, and to bring no more than three months' supply into the UAE.

Culture and etiquette

Despite its glossy Western veneer and apparently liberal ways, it's important to remember that Dubai is an Islamic state, and that visitors are expected to comply with local cultural norms or risk the consequences.

There are a few simple rules to remember if you want to stay out of trouble. During **Ramadan** remember that between dawn and dusk, eating, drinking, smoking or chewing gum in public are a definite no-no, as are singing, dancing and swearing in public (you are, however, free to eat and drink in any of the carefully screened-off dining areas set up in hotels throughout the city, while alcohol is also served discreetly after dark in some places). At any time, public displays of **drunkenness** contravene local law, and could get you locked up. Driving while under any sort of influence is even more of a no-no. Inappropriate public behaviour with members of the opposite sex can result in, at best, embarrassment, or, at worst, a spell in prison. Holding hands or a peck on the cheek is probably just about OK, but any more passionate **displays of affection** are severely frowned upon. **Offensive gestures** are another source of possible danger. Giving someone the finger or even just sticking out your tongue might be considered rude at home but can get you jailed in Dubai.

In terms of general etiquette, except around the hotel pool, **modest dress** is expected of all visitors. Dressing "indecently" is potentially punishable under law (even if actual arrests are extremely rare), although exactly what constitutes indecent attire isn't clearly defined. If you're fortunate enough to spend any time with Emiratis, remember that only the right hand should be used for eating and drinking (this rule also applies in Indian establishments), and don't offer to shake the hand of an Emirati woman unless she extends hers toward you first.

Electricity

UK-style **sockets** with three square pins are the norm (although you might occasionally encounter Indian-style round-pin sockets in budget hotels in Bur Dubai and Deira). The city's **current** runs at 220–240 volts AC, meaning that UK appliances will work directly off the mains supply, although US appliances will probably require a transformer.

Embassies and consulates

Foreign embassies are mainly located in the UAE's capital, Abu Dhabi, although many countries also maintain consulates in Dubai.

Australia Consulate-General, Level 25, BurJuman Business Tower, Khalifa bin Zayed Rd, Bur Dubai 04 508 7100, uae.embassy.gov.au.

Canada Consulate-General, 19th Floor, Emirates Towers (Business Tower), Sheikh Zayed Rd 04 404 8444, www.canadainternational.gc.ca.

Ireland Embassy, 19th St (just off 32nd St), Al Bateen, Abu Dhabi 02 495 8200, dfa.ie/irish-embassy/uae.

New Zealand Embassy, Office 6A, Level 6, Emirates Tower, Sheikh Zayed Road 04 270 0100, mfat.govt.nz.

South Africa Consulate-General, 3rd Floor, New Sharaf Building, Khaleed bin al Waleed St, Bur Dubai 04 397 5222, gov.za.

UK Embassy, Al Seef Rd, Bur Dubai 04 309 4444, ukinuae.fco.gov.uk/en.

US Consulate-General, Corner of Al Seef and Sheikh Khalifa bin Zayed roads, Bur Dubai 04 309 4000, ae.usembassy.gov/.

Health

There are virtually no serious **health risks** in Dubai (unless you include the traffic). The city is well equipped with modern hospitals, while all four- and five-star hotels have English-speaking **doctors** on call 24hr. **Tap water** is safe to drink, while even the city's cheapest curry houses and shwarma cafés maintain good standards of **food hygiene**. The only genuine health concern is the **heat**. Summer temperatures regularly climb into the mid-forties, making sunburn, heatstroke and acute dehydration a real possibility, especially if combined with excessive alcohol consumption. Stay in the shade, and drink lots of water.

Pharmacies can be found all over the city, including a number run by the BinSina chain (binsina.ae) which are open 24hr. There are two main **government hospitals** with emergency departments: Dubai Hospital, between the Corniche and Baraha Street, Deira (04 219 5000); and Rashid Hospital, off Oud Metha Road, near Maktoum Bridge, Oud Metha (04 219 2000). You'll need to pay for treatment, though costs should be recoverable through your travel insurance. **Private hospitals** with emergency departments include the American Hospital, off Oud Metha Road (opposite the *Mövenpick* hotel), Oud Metha (04 337 5000, ahdubai.com), and Emirates Hospital, opposite Jumeirah Beach Park, Jumeirah Beach Road, Jumeirah (800 444 444, emirateshospital.ae).

Internet

Dubai is comprehensively wired, with free Wi-fi available pretty much everywhere, including throughout the metro and tram systems and even (if you have a UAE mobile number) on buses to Sharjah and Abu Dhabi. There are also various Wi-fi hotspots around

Eating price codes

Pricing (in UAE dirhams) is based on a two-course meal for one including a non-alcoholic drink and inclusive of all taxes and service charge.

Dh	under 75dh
DhDh	75–150dh
DhDhDh	150–300dh
DhDhDhDh	over 300dh

the city operated by two telecom companies, Etisalat (Ⓦ etisalat.ae) and Du (Ⓦ du.ae).

Internet access in Dubai is subject to a certain modest amount of **censorship** including a blanket ban on anything remotely pornographic, plus gambling and dating sites, and pages which are considered religiously or culturally offensive.

LGBTQ+ travellers

Dubai is one of the world's less friendly destinations for LGBTQ+ communities. Homosexuality is illegal under UAE law, with punishments of up to ten years in prison – a useful summary of the present legal situation and recent prosecutions can be found at Ⓦ en.wikipedia.org/wiki/LGBT_rights_in_the_United_Arab_Emirates. Despite this, a very clandestine gay scene exists, attracting both foreigners and Arabs from even less permissive cities around the Gulf, although such parties in Dubai are usually only publicised via social media and word of mouth. Relevant websites are routinely censored within the UAE, so you'll probably have to do your online research before you arrive – check out the useful guide at Ⓦ nomadicboys.com – Is Dubai Safe for Gay Travellers?

Lost property

For major items of lost property, try asking at the nearest local police station. If you accidentally leave something in a taxi, call the RTA Contact Centre on Ⓣ 800 9090.

Money

The UAE's currency is the **dirham** (abbreviated "dh" or "AED"), subdivided into 100 fils. The dirham is pegged against the US dollar at the rate of $1=3.6725dh; other **exchange rates** at the time of writing were £1=5dh, €1=4dh. **Notes** come in 5dh, 10dh, 20dh, 50dh, 100dh, 200dh, 500dh and 1000dh denominations; there are also 2dh, 1dh, 50 fils and 25 fils coins.

There are plenty of **ATMs** all over the city which accept foreign Visa and MasterCards. All the big shopping malls have at least a few ATMs, as do some large hotels and almost all banks. All will also change **foreign cash**, and there are also plenty of **moneychangers**, including the reputable Al Ansari Exchange, which has branches all over the city (see Ⓦ alansariexchange.com/en/branches).

Opening hours

Dubai traditionally ran on an Islamic rather than a Western schedule, meaning that the city operated according to a basic **five-day working week** running Sunday to Thursday, with Friday as the Islamic holy day and Friday and Saturday as the "weekend". Recent years have seen considerable changes to this pattern however, and the city now increasingly follows the international Monday to Friday norm, although a few places still remain closed on Friday mornings. **Shops** in **malls** generally open daily from 10am to 10pm, and until midnight on

Emergency numbers

Ambulance ⓣ 998
Fire ⓣ 997
Police ⓣ 999

Friday and Saturday (and sometimes Thursday as well); shops in **souks** follow a similar pattern, though many places close for a siesta between around 1pm and 4pm depending on the whim of the owner. Most **restaurants** open daily for lunch and dinner (although some more upmarket hotel restaurants open for dinner only). **Pubs** tend to open daily from around noon until 2am; some **hotel bars** stay open slightly later from around 6pm until 2/3am.

Phones

The **country code** for the UAE is ⓣ 971. The **city code** for Dubai is ⓣ 04; Abu Dhabi is ⓣ 02; Sharjah is ⓣ 06; Al Ain is ⓣ 03. Numbers prefixed ⓣ 05 are local mobile numbers, with the Eitisalat code of ⓣ 050 probably the most widely used. Phone numbers prefixed ⓣ 800 are toll free. To **call abroad from the UAE**, dial ⓣ 00, followed by your country code and the number itself (minus its initial zero). To call Dubai from abroad, dial your international access code, then ⓣ 971 (country code) followed by the local landline or mobile number minus the initial "0".

Post

The two most convenient **post offices** for visitors are the Al Musalla Post Office (Sat–Thurs 7.30am–3pm) at Al Fahidi Roundabout, opposite the *Arabian Tea House Café* in Bur Dubai; and the Deira Post Office on Al Sabkha Road (Sat–Thurs 8am–8pm), near the intersection with Baniyas Road. Airmail letters to Europe, the US and Australia cost 6dh (postcards 4dh).

Smoking

Smoking is banned in Dubai in the vast majority of indoor public places, including offices, malls, cafés and restaurants, as well as public outdoor spaces including parks and beaches. It is, however, still permitted indoors at most bars and pubs, although a few places have declared themselves non-smoking. Many **hotels** now provide non-smoking rooms or non-smoking floors – and an increasing number of places (particularly more upmarket establishments) have banned smoking completely. During Ramadan, never smoke in public places in daylight hours.

Time

Dubai (and the rest of the UAE) runs on **Gulf Standard Time**. This is 4hr ahead of GMT, 3hr ahead of BST, 9hr ahead of North American Eastern Standard Time, 12hr ahead of North American Western Standard Time, 6hr behind Australian Eastern Standard Time, and 8hr behind New Zealand Standard Time. There is no daylight-saving time in Dubai.

Tipping and taxes

Room rates at the city's hotels are subject to five percent VAT, a seven percent "municipality fee" and a tourism fee of 7–20dh per day depending on the hotel's star rating – while some places also add a ten percent **service charge.** Taxes and charges are usually included in quoted prices but always check beforehand or you may find your bill has suddenly inflated by over twenty percent. Menu prices in most restaurants also usually include VAT and municipality fee, plus a ten percent service charge (though this isn't necessarily passed on to the waiters themselves); whether you wish to leave an additional **tip** is entirely your decision.

Tourist information

There's almost no on-the-ground visitor information in Dubai – and not a single proper tourist office anywhere in the city. Online, the official government website (visitdubai.com) is worth a browse, although the best resource is the lively *Time Out Dubai*, whether in magazine form – it's published weekly and available at bookshops all over the city – or online (timeoutdubai.com). It carries comprehensive listings about pretty much everything going on in Dubai and is particularly good for information about the constantly changing nightlife scene, including club, restaurant and bar promotions and new openings.

Travelling with children

Dubai has a vast array of attractions for children, although many come with hefty price tags attached. Most of the city's beach hotels have their own in-house **kids' clubs**, providing free childcare (usually catering for ages 4–12), while most larger shopping malls have dedicated kids' play areas. Most hotels can arrange **babysitting** services for a fee. Attractions designed especially for kids include:

Children's City

Creek Park, Oud Metha (04 334 0808, childrencity.dm.gov.ae; Dubai Healthcare City metro).

Occupying an eye-catching series of brightly coloured red and blue buildings in Creek Park, Children's City is aimed at kids aged 2–15, with a subtle educational slant and various galleries with fun interactive exhibits. 15dh, children 3–15 years 10dh; under-2s free; family ticket for two adults and two children 40dh. Mon–Fri 9am–8pm, Sat & Sun 2–8pm.

Dubai Safari

Al Warqa, Hatta Rd (dubaisafari.ae).

Around 20km (12 miles) inland from the centre, this big new state-of-the-art safari park is home to around three thousand animals, from lions and rhinos to oryx and Arabian wolves. From 50dh, ages 3-12 20dh. Daily 9am–5pm.

Ferrari World

Yas Island, Abu Dhabi (02 496 8000, ferrariworldabudhabi.com).

The blockbuster attraction at Abu Dhabi's Yas Island (see page 94), the "world's biggest indoor theme park" offers a wide range of Ferrari-themed rides and displays which will appeal both to kids and grown-ups. Adults and children over 1.3m 345dh; under 1.3m 265dh; under-3s free. Daily 11am–8pm.

KidZania

Second floor, Dubai Mall (kidzania.ae; Burj Khalifa/Dubai Mall metro).

Innovative edutainment attraction based on an imaginary city where the kids are in charge. Children get the chance to dress up and role-play from 75 different grown-up professions and even earn their own money en route. Ages 17+ 80dh; ages 4–16 from 260dh; ages 2–3 110dh; under-1s free. Daily 10am–11pm.

Legoland Dubai & Legoland Water Park

Dubai Parks and Resorts, Jebel Ali (04 820 0000, legoland.com/dubai).

Dubai offshoot of the famous theme-park franchise with plenty of brick-tastic fun, plus attached Lego-themed waterpark. From 295dh, or 335dh with waterpark. Daily 10am–6pm.

Madame Tussauds Dubai

Bluewaters Island, Dubai Marina (04 873 3042, madametussauds.com/dubai).

Public holidays

There are nine public holidays in Dubai: three have fixed dates, while the other five shift annually according to the Islamic calendar (falling around eleven days earlier from year to year).

New Year's Day Jan 1.
Milad un Nabi (Birth of the Prophet Mohammed) Estimated dates: 15 Sept 2024, 5 Sept 2025, 26 Aug 2026, 15 Aug, 2027
Eid ul Fitr (the end of Ramadan) Estimated dates: 10 April 2024, 31 March 2025, 20 March 2026, 10 March 2027.
Arafat (Haj) Day Estimated dates: 15 June 2024, 5 June 2025, 26 May 2026, 16 May 2027.
Eid al Adha (the Festival of the Sacrifice) Estimated dates: 16 June 2024, 7 June 2025, 26 May 2026, 17 May 2027.
Al Hijra (Islamic New Year) Estimated dates: 7 July 2024, 27 June 2025, 6 June 2026, 25 May 2027
Commemoration Day (Martyrs' Day) 30 November.
National Day 2 December.

Have tea with Queen Elizabeth II or create your own Bollywood dance routine at this local branch of the famous London waxwork extravaganza. 145dh. Daily noon to 10pm.

Motiongate Dubai

Dubai Parks and Resorts, Jebel Ali (T04 820 0000, W motiongatedubai.com).

Glitzy new theme park with movie-inspired rides and attractions for all ages. 295dh. Daily noon to 9pm.

Penguin Encounter

Ski Dubai. Mall of the Emirates T 04 409 4000, W skidxb.com.

Get up close to some of Ski Dubai's resident Gentoo and King penguins in these 40 minute "interactive penguin encounters", including close-up underwater viewing and the chance to interact with at least two of the little critters at close quarters. Warm clothing and gloves provided. From 230dh. Daily 10am to midnight.

Festivals and events

Dubai hosts a number of world-class annual festivals showcasing film, music and the visual arts, while neighbouring Abu Dhabi also stages a number of leading cultural and sporting events. For a complete listing of events in the city, see W dubaicalendar.ae.

Dubai Marathon

Mid-Jan W dubaimarathon.org.
Top distance runners battle it out.

Dubai Shopping Festival

Six weeks in Dec-Jan
Shops citywide offer all sorts of sales bargains, with discounts of up to 75 percent, while the big mega malls lay on entertainment and children's events.

Dubai Desert Classic

Four days in Jan/Feb
W dubaidesertclassic.com.
Major event on the PGA European Tour held at the Emirates Golf Club and attracting leading stars.

Traditional dhow racing

Feb W dimc.ae.
Traditional wooden dhows under sail at the Dubai International Marine Club in Dubai Marina.

Taste of Dubai

Three days in mid-Feb
tasteofdubaifestival.com.
Live cookery exhibitions at Dubai Media City by local and visiting international celebrity chefs.

Dubai Duty Free Tennis Championships

Two weeks in late Feb/early March
Established fixture on the international tennis calendar at the Dubai Tennis Stadium in Garhoud, pulling in top male and female players.

Abu Dhabi Desert Challenge

One week in Feb/March
abudhabidesertchallenge.com.
Rally drivers, bikers and quad-bikers will enjoy the thrills as they race each other across the desert.

Art Dubai

Four days in March artdubai.ae.
Some 75 galleries from around the world exhibit at Madinat Jumeirah.

Dubai World Cup

March.
The world's richest horse race, with a massive $12 million in prize money at stake, held at annually at the Meydan Racecourse.

Dubai Food Festival

Two weeks in late April/early May
Citywide event with foodie bargains galore.

Dubai Summer Surprises

Mid-June to mid-September
Mainly mall-based event with shopping bargains on offer and lots of live children's entertainment.

Ramadan

Estimated dates: 11 March to 9 April 2024, 1–30 March 2025, 18 Feb to 19 March 2026, 8 Feb 9 March 2027
The Islamic holy month of Ramadan is observed with great care in Dubai. Muslims are required to fast from dawn to dusk, and as a tourist you are expected publicly to observe these strictures (see page 113). Fasting ends at dusk, at which point the city springs to life in a celebratory round of eating, drinking and socializing known as Iftar ("The Breaking of the Fast"). The atmosphere is particularly exuberant during Eid ul Fitr, the day marking the end of Ramadan, which erupts in an explosion of festivity. Precise dates for Ramadan change annually.

Eid al Adha

Estimated dates: 16 June 2024, 7 June 2025, 26 May 2026, 17 May 2027
Falling approximately 70 days after the end of Ramadan, the "Festival of the Sacrifice" celebrates the willingness of Ibrahim to sacrifice his son Ismail at the command of God.

Abu Dhabi F1 Grand Prix

Three days in Nov
yasmarinacircuit.com.
The Gulf's premier sporting event, held annually at the spectacular Yas Marina Circuit.

Dubai World Tour Championship

Four days in Nov facebook.com/DPWorldTourChampionship.
Held at the Earth course, Jumeirah Golf Estates, this is the showpiece finale of the European Tour's season-long "Race to Dubai".

Dubai Rugby Sevens

Three days in late Nov/early Dec
dubairugby7s.com.
Annual IRB Sevens World Series tournament at Dubai's Sevens stadium, accompanied by some of the city's most raucous partying.

Dubai International Film Festival

One week in mid-Dec ⓦ facebook. com/DubaiFilmFestival. International art-house films are shown during this festival, with a particular focus on home-grown work. There are usually a few well-known celebs in attendance.

National Day

Dec 2
Independence Day is celebrated with a raft of citywide events.

Chronology

c.5000 BC Earliest human settlement in the southern Gulf.

500–600 AD The United Arab Emirates region becomes part of an extensive trade network dominated by the Sassanian (Iranian) empire; settlement of Jumeirah area.

c.630 Arrival of Islam.

751 and onwards The southern Gulf experiences a major boom in maritime trade following the shifting of the Islamic caliphate from Damascus to Baghdad.

1580 First European reference to Dubai, by the Venetian pearl merchant Gaspero Balbi.

1820 Britain signs a series of treaties (or "truces") with various Gulf rulers, whose territories are henceforth known as the Trucial States.

1833 Around a thousand Bani Yas tribesmen from Abu Dhabi take control of Dubai under the leadership of Maktoum bin Buti.

1835 Britain formally recognizes Dubai and enters into treaty with it.

1841 Settlement of Deira begins. Over the next few decades the town grows rapidly, attracting a cosmopolitan population of Arabs, Iranians, Indians and Pakistanis to set up residence in the region.

1894 Dubai declared a free port by Sheikh Maktoum bin Hasher. Iranian merchants begin arriving in the city.

1929 onwards Gradual collapse of the pearl trade following the Great Depression and Japanese discovery of artificial pearl culturing.

1958 Death of Sheikh Saeed, succeeded by his son Sheikh Rashid.

1960 Dubai International Airport is opened.

1960–61 The Creek is dredged, establishing Dubai as the southern Gulf's major port.

1963 The first bridge across the Creek – Maktoum Bridge – is opened.

1966 Oil is discovered in the offshore Fateh field.

1971 The British withdraw from the Trucial States, which are re-formed as the United Arab Emirates. Opening of Port Rashid.

1970s and 1980s Oil revenues are used to diversify Dubai's industrial base and create massive new infrastructure projects, such as Jebel Ali Port and Free Zone (1983), and the World Trade Centre (1979).

1990 Death of Sheikh Rashid; Sheikh Maktoum becomes ruler of Dubai, though Crown Prince Sheikh

Mohammed also exerts increasing influence over the city's development.

1996 Dubai Shopping Festival held for the first time.

1998 Opening of the Burj al Arab.

2006 Death of popular leader Sheikh Maktoum; Sheikh Mohammed becomes ruler.

2008 Credit crunch hits Dubai; emirate teeters on edge of bankruptcy; many major projects cancelled or mothballed.

2010 Opening of Burj Khalifa, the world's tallest building.

2016 Opening of the Dubai Water Canal.

2020 The UAE launches the "Hope" spacecraft, becoming only the fifth country to successfully land a probe on Mars.

2021–22 Dubai hosts the covid-delayed World Expo 2020.

2023 Planned opening of the world's first "floating hotel", the Kempinski Floating Palace, off Jumeirah Beach.

Language

Language in Dubai is as complicated as the ethnic patchwork of people who inhabit the city. The city's official language is **Arabic**, spoken by nearly a third of the population, including local Emiratis, other Gulf Arabs and various Arabic-speaking expats from countries like Lebanon, Syria, Jordan and further afield. **Hindi** and **Urdu** are the mother tongues of many of the city's enormous number of Indian and Pakistani expats, although other Indian languages, most notably Malayalam, the native tongue of Kerala, as well as Tamil and Sinhalese (the majority language of Sri Lanka), are also spoken. Other Asian languages are also common, most notably **Tagalog**, the first language of the city's large Filipino community.

In practice, the city's most widely understood language is actually **English** (even if most speak it only as a second or third language), which serves as a link between all the city's various ethnic groups, as well as the principal language of the European expat community and the business and tourism sectors. Pretty much everyone in Dubai speaks at least a little English (ironically, even local Dubaians are now forced to revert to this foreign language in many of their everyday dealings in their own city).

Knowing the ethnic origin of the person you're speaking to is obviously the most important thing if you do attempt to strike out into a foreign tongue – speaking Arabic to an Indian taxi driver or a Filipina waitress is obviously a complete waste of time. The bottom line is that few of the people you come into contact with in Dubai will be Arabic-speakers.

Useful Arabic words and phrases

Hello (formal) a'salaam alaykum (response: wa alaykum a'salaam)
Hello (informal) marhaba/ahlan wasahlan
Good morning sabah al kheer
Good evening masaa al kheer
Good night (to a man/ tisbah al kher/ **woman)** tisbahi al kher
Goodbye ma'assalama
Yes na'am/aiwa
No la
Please (to a man/ minfadlack/**woman)** minfadlick
Excuse me afwan
Thank you shukran

You're welcome afwan
Sorry afwan
OK n'zayn
How much? bikaim?
Do you speak English? teh ki ingelezi?
I don't speak Arabic ma ah'ki arabi
I understand ana fahim (fem: ana fahma)
I don't understand ana ma fahim (fem: ana ma fahma)
My name is ... Ismi ...
What is your name? Sho ismak?
God willing! Inshallah
I'm British ana Britani
...Irish ...Irlandee
...American ...Amerikanee
...Canadian ...Canadee
...Australian ...Ostralee
...from New Zealand ...Noozeelandee
Where are you from? min wayn inta?
Where is? wayn?
in fi
near/far gareeb/ba'eed
here/there hina/hunak
open/closed maftooh/mseeker
big/small kabeer/saghir
old/new kadeem/jadeed
day/night yoom/layl
today/tomorrow al yoom/bokra
perhaps mumkin
No problem ma fi mushkila
Not possible mish mumkin
I don't speak Arabic ma'atkallam arabi (or just la arabiya)
Leave me alone! imshi!

Numbers

1 wahid
2 ithnayn
3 theletha
4 arba'a
5 khamsa
6 sitta
7 saba'a
8 themanya
9 tissa
10 ashra
20 aishreen
30 thelatheen
40 arba'aeen
50 khamseen
100 maya
1000 elf

Food glossary

The traditional Middle Eastern meal consists of a wide selection of small dishes known as **mezze** (or *meze*) shared between a number of diners. Most or all of the following dishes, dips and other ingredients are found in the city's better Middle Eastern (or "Lebanese", as they are usually described) restaurants and cafés, although note that vagaries in the transliteration from Arabic script to English can result in considerable variations in spelling.

arayes slices of pitta bread stuffed with spiced meat
baba ghanouj all-purpose dip made from grilled aubergine (eggplant) mixed with ingredients like tomato, onion, lemon juice and garlic
burghul cracked wheat, often used in Middle Eastern dishes such as tabbouleh
falafel deep-fried balls of crushed chickpeas mixed with spices
fatayer miniature triangular pastries, usually filled with either cheese or spinach
fatteh dishes containing pieces of fried or roasted bread
fattoush salad made of tomatoes, cucumber, lettuce and mint mixed up with crispy little squares of deep-fried flatbread
foul madamas smooth dip made from fava beans (*foul*) blended with lemon juice, chillis and olive oil
halloumi grilled cheese
hammour common Gulf fish which often crops up on local menus; a bit like cod
humous crushed chickpeas blended with tahini, garlic and lemon
jebne white cheese
kibbeh small ovals of deep-fried minced lamb mixed with cracked wheat and spices
kushari classic Egyptian dish featuring a mix of rice, lentils, noodles, macaroni and fried onion, topped with tomato sauce
labneh thick, creamy Arabian yoghurt, often flavoured with garlic or mint

loubia salad of green beans with tomatoes and onion
moutabal a slightly creamier version of *baba ghanouj*, thickened using yoghurt or tahini
mulukhiyah soup/stew with a characteristically slimy texture, made from boiled *mulukhiyah* leaves
saj Lebanese style of thin, round flatbread
saj manakish (or *mana'eesh*) pieces of *saj* sprinkled with herbs and oil – a kind of Middle Eastern mini-pizza
sambousek miniature pastries, filled with meat or cheese and then fried
sharkaseya chicken served in a creamy walnut sauce
shish taouk basic chicken kebab, with small pieces of meat grilled on a skewer and often served with garlic sauce
shisha waterpipe (also known as hubbly-bubbly). Tobacco is filtered through the glass water-container at the base of the pipe
shwarma chicken or lamb kebabs, cut in narrow strips off meat roasted on a spit and served wrapped in flatbread with salad
tabbouleh finely chopped mixture of tomato, mint and cracked wheat
tahini paste made from sesame seeds
waraq aynab vine leaves stuffed with a mixture of rice and meat
zaatar a widely used seasoning made from a mixture of dried thyme (or oregano), salt and sesame seeds
zatoon olives

Glossary

abbeya black, full-length women's traditional robe
abra small boat used to ferry passengers
attar traditional perfume
bahar sea
barasti palm thatch used to construct traditional houses
bayt/bait house
burj tower
dar house
dhow generic term loosely used to describe all types of traditional wooden Arabian boat
dishdasha see *kandoura*
Eid ul Fitr festival celebrating the end of Ramadan (see page 119)
falaj traditional irrigation technique used to water date plantations, with water along tiny canals
funduk hotel
ghutra men's headscarf, usually white or red-and-white check
haj pilgrimage to Mecca
hosn/hisn fort
iftar the breaking of the fast during Ramadan
iqal the rope-like black cords used to keep the *ghutra* on the head (traditionally used to tie together the legs of camels to stop them running off)
jebel hill or mountain
kandoura the full-length traditional robe worn by Gulf Arabs (also known as *dishdashas*). A decorative tassel, known as the *farokha* (or *tarboush*), often hangs from the collar. A long robe, or *basht*, is sometimes worn over the *dishdasha* on formal occasions, denoting the authority of the wearer
Al Khaleej the Gulf (translated locally as the Arabian Gulf, never as the Persian Gulf)
khanjar traditional curved dagger, usually made of silver
Al Khor the Creek
majlis meeting/reception room in a traditional Arabian house; the place where local or family problems were discussed and decisions taken
mashrabiya projecting window protected by a carved wooden latticework screen – although the term is often loosely used to describe any kind of elaborately carved latticework screen
masjid mosque
mina port
nakheel palm tree
oud Arabian lute; also the name of a key ingredient in Arabian perfumes derived from agarwood
qasr palace or castle
qibla the direction of Mecca, usually indicated by a sign or sticker in most hotel rooms in the city (and in mosques by a recessed niche known as the mihrab)
Ramadan see page 119
shayla women's black headscarf, worn with an *abbeya*
wadi dry river bed or valley

Publishing Information

Fourth edition 2023

Distribution
UK, Ireland and Europe
Apa Publications (UK) Ltd; sales@roughguides.com
United States and Canada
Ingram Publisher Services; ips@ingramcontent.com
Australia and New Zealand
Booktopia; retailer@booktopia.com.au
Worldwide
Apa Publications (UK) Ltd; sales@roughguides.com

Special Sales, Content Licensing and CoPublishing
Rough Guides can be purchased in bulk quantities at discounted prices. We can create special editions, personalised jackets and corporate imprints tailored to your needs. sales@roughguides.com.
roughguides.com

Printed in Czech Republic

This book was produced using **Typefi** automated publishing software.

A catalogue record for this book is available from the British Library
The publishers and authors have done their best to ensure the accuracy and currency of all the information in **Pocket Rough Guide Dubai**, however, they can accept no responsibility for any loss, injury, or inconvenience sustained by any traveller as a result of information or advice contained in the guide.

Rough Guide Credits

Editor: Kate Drynan, Philippa MacKenzie
Cartography: Katie Bennett
Picture editor: Tom Smyth
Layout: Pradeep Thapliyal
Original design: Richard Czapnik
Head of DTP and Pre-Press: Rebeka Davies
Head of Publishing: Sarah Clark

Help us update

We've gone to a lot of effort to ensure that this edition of the **Pocket Rough Guide Dubai** is accurate and up-to-date. However, things change – places get "discovered", opening hours are notoriously fickle, restaurants and rooms raise prices or lower standards. If you feel we've got it wrong or left something out, we'd like to know, and if you can remember the address, the price, the hours, the phone number, so much the better.

Please send your comments with the subject line "**Pocket Rough Guide Dubai Update**" to mail@uk.roughguides.com. We'll credit all contributions and send a copy of the next edition (or any other Rough Guide if you prefer) for the very best emails.

Photo Credits

(Key: T-top; C-centre; B-bottom; L-left; R-right)

Abdallah Elabry/Dubai Tourism 14T, 30
Address Hotels + Resorts 58
Antonie Robertson/One&Only Royal Mirage 78
Chris Cypert/Jumeirah Media Library 19B, 70
Getty Images 14B
iStock 11T, 13B, 16T, 18C, 38, 50, 62, 72, 106/107
Jumeirah Media Library 96/97
Kerzner International 15B
Neil Corder/Four Points by Sheraton 5
Neil Scott Corder 80
Nicolas Dumont 79, 81
Shutterstock 1, 2T, 2BL, 2C, 2BR, 4, 10, 12/13T, 12B, 13C, 18C, 19T, 20T, 21C, 22/23, 25, 31, 32, 45, 54, 55, 63, 64, 71, 89
Tim Draper/Rough Guides 6, 15T, 16B, 17B, 17T, 18T, 18B, 19C, 20C, 20B, 21T, 21B, 24, 28, 35, 37, 40, 41, 43, 47, 48, 49, 51, 53, 56, 59, 67, 69, 73, 75, 76, 77, 83, 85, 87, 90, 91, 93, 94

Cover: Dubai Frame **Grisha Bruev/Shutterstock**

Index

INDEX